A REMARKABLE DISCOVERY AND AN UNSOLVED MYSTERY

Pawnbroking in thentury,
with a case stu   llier

A Remarkable Discovery
And An Unsolved Mystery

Christine Pinder

Carnegie Heritage Centre
Kingston upon Hull
2022

A Remarkable Discovery

Christine Pinder asserts the moral right to be identified as the author of this work.

The first edition of this work was published 2022
by
Carnegie Heritage Centre Ltd.
342 Anlaby Road, Hull, HU3 6JA

ISBN 978-0-9555569-8-2

British Library in Publication Data
A catalogue record for this book is available from the British Library

Published by Carnegie Heritage Centre Ltd.

Printed by Dolman Scott
www.dolmanscott.com

Table of Contents

	Page
A Remarkable and Mysterious Discovery	7
Hull in the Second Half of the Nineteenth Century: Prosperity and Poverty	10
Pawnbroking Nationally From Around 1850 to the Present Day	20
Pawnbroking in Hull From Around 1850 to the Present Day	25
Robert Collier's Personal Life	25
Collier's Business Career	36
Collier's Will and the Estate He Left	50
The Unsolved Mystery: why were 6,871 pawn tickets hidden up the chimney in Collier's South Street premises?	55
Reflections	58
Appendix: an analysis of the information on the 6,871 pawn tickets that were hidden up the chimney in Collier's South Street premises	58
Sources Used	65
Acknowledgements	68
The Author	68

A REMARKABLE AND MYSTERIOUS DISCOVERY

In the second half of the nineteenth century pawnbroking businesses thrived in Hull, with many people living in poverty and surviving from week to week by pawning their belongings. One such pawnbroking business was that of Robert Collier (1842-1913), who at one time owned three pawnbroking shops in the centre of Hull.

Collier's main shop was in South Street, which in the later 1800s ran between Paragon Street and West Street, before Jameson Street was built in 1903. The building that was Collier's shop still stands today, and it was here in mid-2020 that a remarkable discovery was made which became the inspiration for this book. The building was being converted into apartments by builder Steve Constable and his team, and when they were knocking out the chimney stack, out fell onto the builders' heads nearly 6,900 pawn tickets (exact figure 6,871), which had been hidden (apparently deliberately) as far up the chimney as possible, at loft level; they were threaded together on lengths of string. The tickets were dated from 1887 to 1896, with approximately 96% (6,571 individual tickets) being from the years 1888, 1889 and 1890. Because the tickets had been hidden up the chimney, they were extremely sooty but very well preserved, as they had remained dry in the warmth generated by many years of coal fires. It was amazing to think that most of the tickets had been hidden up this chimney for around 130 years, and very intriguing indeed to speculate about why they ended up there in the first place; the latter will be discussed later in this book.

Following this unexpected and very mysterious discovery, builder Steve asked on Facebook if anyone was interested in having the tickets, and that was where Christine Pinder, the author of this book, came in. She contacted Steve, who agreed to hand over the tickets to the Carnegie Heritage Centre, where Christine volunteers. A dedicated team of Carnegie volunteers started painstakingly separating the tickets (whilst getting very dirty!) and entering them onto a spreadsheet, so that Christine could analyse their contents. During this process it soon became clear that the tickets would be a fascinating and invaluable primary source of historical information, painting a unique and vivid picture of pawnbroking in Hull in the second half of the nineteenth century, as well as of the social and economic conditions at that time. It was therefore decided to disseminate the findings from Christine's analysis of the tickets to the wider public, and this book is the result.

The pawn tickets as found by builder Steve Constable, threaded together on lengths of string (photograph taken by the author).

Samples of the 6,871 pawn tickets (photograph taken by the author)

Whilst the tickets were being indexed, Christine researched the life and business of pawnbroker Robert Collier, as well as the wider social and economic context in which he operated. Therefore, this book is effectively an outline of pawnbroking nationally and in Hull in the second half of the nineteenth century, using Robert Collier's pawnbroking business as a case study, whilst drawing on findings from the analysis of the 6,871 pawn tickets found hidden up the South Street chimney (see Appendix).

The book first puts pawnbroking in the second half of the nineteenth century into the context of the socio-economic conditions in Hull at that time, covering the city's economy and industries, workers' wages, the cost of living and workers' living conditions. The book then goes on to look at pawnbroking during the same period, including the main principles, the relevant national legislation, and the extent of pawnbroking in Hull.

Following these sections the book covers the life and business career of pawnbroker Robert Collier, including comparisons with two other pawnbrokers who owned shops in Hull during the same period as Collier. There is then a consideration of possible answers to the intriguing question of why 6,871 pawn tickets belonging to Robert Collier were apparently deliberately hidden up the chimney in his South Street premises.

The detailed analysis of the pawn tickets is in an appendix; the text of the book draws on the results of this analysis throughout, and the detail in the Appendix can be referred to as necessary.

Please note that the 6,871 pawn tickets can be viewed at the Carnegie Heritage Centre, contact details on the back cover of this book.

Notes on the currency figures quoted in this book

Until decimalisation in February 1971, the United Kingdom used "pounds, shillings and pence" (£sd) currency, now known colloquially as "old money". This is therefore used in the text of this book and in the pawn tickets analysis (see Appendix). £sd currency was divided into pounds (£), shillings (s) and pence (d), as follows:

- Two half pence (1/2d) in one pence (1d)
- Twelve pence (12d) in one shilling (1s)
- Twenty shillings (20s or 240d) in one pound (£1).

Throughout this book the author has put in brackets after the £sd currency amounts the approximate equivalent in today's decimal currency, using Webster's United Kingdom Inflation Calculator (see Sources Used). All equivalents were calculated from the year 1889 (the year given on 57% of the total number of pawn tickets) to 25th August 2022, so they are directly comparable with each other. Please note that numbers and percentages have been rounded up or down for simplicity, so may appear inconsistent in places.

HULL IN THE SECOND HALF OF THE NINETEENTH CENTURY: PROSPERITY AND POVERTY

Economy and industries

NOTE: unless otherwise stated, the information in this section is adapted from Allison (1969).

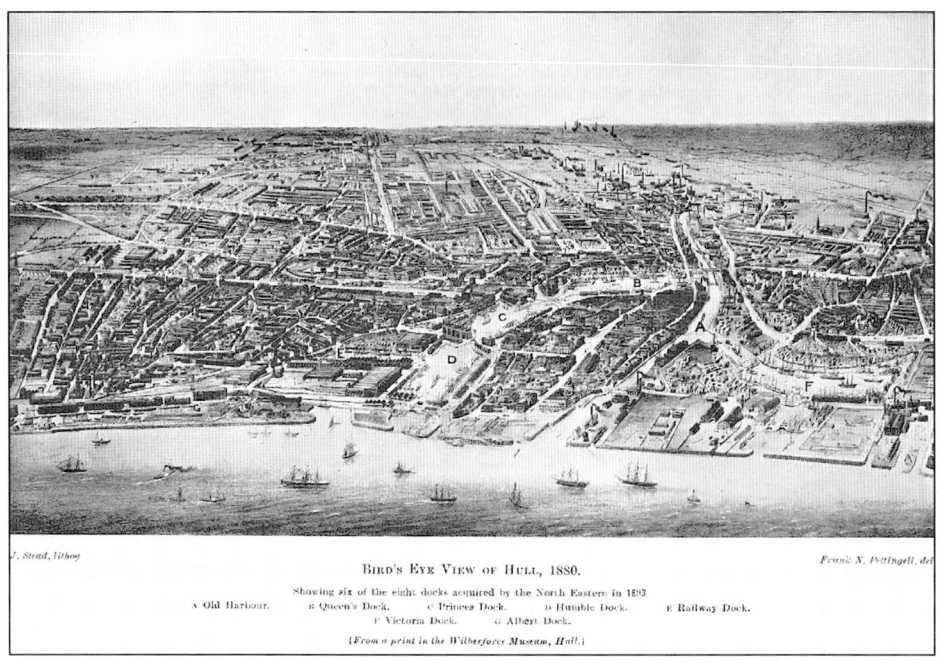

Bird's Eye View of Hull, 1880 (Pettingell)

Hull's population grew rapidly in the later 1800s; in 1861, the population of the Hull and Sculcoates Registration Districts was 109,000, growing to 178,000 by 1881 and to 239,000 by 1901. This growth stemmed largely from the development of port related industries, as Hull became Britain's third port. In turn, as these industries

River Hull from North Bridge c.1880 (F.S. Smith in Ketchell, 1990)

developed there was substantial migration into Hull from the countryside and also from Ireland and Lancashire, leading to overcrowding of the available housing (discussed in detail later).

By 1900, Hull had nine purpose built docks and their associated railways dealing with both goods and passengers, as overseas links and trade grew. Hull's other major industries included shipbuilding, paint manufacturing, oil seed crushing and cotton milling. North Sea trawling was also developing (Markham (2003) states that by 1895, there was a fishing workforce of around 5,000), along with associated industries such as fish curing, ice making and cod liver oil production. This was a very diverse range of industries in comparison with other Yorkshire towns of a similar size. Also during the later 1800s, large companies began developing which would eventually become internationally well-known, including Reckitt and Sons (later Reckitt and Colman, Reckitt Benckiser, RB and now Reckitt), Joseph Rank's flour mills (later Rank Hovis McDougall Limited), and Smith and Nephew, manufacturers of wound care treatments and personal care products. In turn, out of these developments emerged a class of nouveau riche industrialists and entrepreneurs, whose demands for high fashion and for building and furnishing their large, newly built homes were catered for by many shopkeepers and tradesmen.

Despite these growing industries, during the latter half of the nineteenth century a good proportion of the jobs available were often either casual or seasonal, or had few prospects; examples of such jobs were those for dock workers and seamen. Neither were there many jobs for women in Hull's industries, apart from in the cotton mills. Hand in hand with this went low wages, even for jobs that were relatively regular, such as those in the 1880s involving working on the city's large scale public improvement schemes, including road widening and the building of bridges over the River Hull. Add to this the mechanisation of many industrial processes during the Industrial Revolution, with fewer jobs available as a result, and a contrasting picture emerges of the wealth of the industrialists and entrepreneurs against the poverty endured by the working classes, even when they were in work.

Workers' wages

During 1889, the Hull Daily Mail (British Newspaper Archive) reported the considerable industrial unrest in the city at that time, with workers in several sectors demanding higher wages; this was also happening nationally. In February and June of that year there were disputes about firemen's and seamen's wages in Hull, and in February the Hull Daily Mail reported that their wage of £3 5s (£463.75) a month "was not enough for men and their wives and families to live upon". After the June strike, these workers were signing on to ships at the union rate of £1 10s 4d (£216.86) a week, a considerable increase from their previous wage. Also in June 1889 there was a strike by those working in shipbuilding, for example iron workers and engineers, when 1,500 men came out, demanding higher wages; Earle's Shipyard (on the banks of the River Humber) was particularly affected by this.

As mentioned above, employment for dock workers tended to be casual or seasonal; it must also be borne in mind that there was no benefits system until 1948, when a comprehensive system of social security came into being following the Beveridge Report of 1942. In Collier's time therefore, workers received no money when they were out of work. In December 1889 the Hull Daily Mail (British Newspaper Archive) detailed the wages paid to dock workers by the famous Hull based shipping company the Wilson Line (later the Ellerman's Wilson Line). Dock labourers loading the ships earned 4s 6d (£32.14) a day and runner men earned 5s (£35.75) a day; dock labourers unloading the ships earned 6d (£3.54) an hour and runner men earned 7d (£4.13) an hour.

An example of seasonal wage fluctuations reported in the Hull Daily Mail (British Newspaper Archive) in 1889 was that of plumbers, who earned 8d (£4.72) an hour. During the summer they worked 36 weeks of 53 hours a week, and during the winter they worked the remaining 16 weeks of only 47 hours, a difference of approximately 4s (£28.60) a week.

The cost of living

To put the wages outlined above into context, it is helpful to look at the cost of living during Collier's time. Knowles (1888) came up with some average costs for staple items for a family of two in England; however, it must be noted that these are averages and may vary between different regions of the country. Also, it is likely that some poorer people did not eat or use some of these items, and it can perhaps be assumed that in the area around Collier's South Street shop, many households consisted of not only two parents, but also several children; they might also have been multigenerational households. Nevertheless, Knowles' figures give some idea of the cost of living for a family of two, which with care can be scaled up for larger families.

All the following figures for food staples were per week: flour 2s (£14.30), milk 10½d (£6.20), bread (ten loaves) 2s 3 ½d (£16.37), meat 4s (£28.60), butter 1s (£7.15), tea (1/2 lb) 1s (£7.15), sugar (4 lbs) 10d (£5.90), vegetables (18 lbs) 1s (£7.15). Similarly, Knowles averaged the weekly cost of non-food items as follows: candles 1d (59p), coal (1 cwt) 1s 3d (£8.92), soap (1½ lbs) 6d (£3.54), soda and starch 5d (£2.95), rent 5s 6d (£39.29).

Knowles (1888) also gave the average costs of items of clothing. These were for new items of clothing, but it should be acknowledged that many such items would be passed down through the family, and only bought new when absolutely necessary. Knowles' figures included: weekday suit £2 (£286), Sunday suit £2 10s (£357.50), pair of socks 1s 10p (£13.05), pair of boots 10s 6d (£75.04), under vest 2s 2d (£15.48), flannel shirt 3s (£21.45). The pawn tickets analysis (see Appendix) shows that the ten most pawned items at Collier's South Street shop were all clothing, with the exception of face flannels; these top ten made up 66% of the total items pawned (approximately 8,841). It may be that poorer people had relatively little to pawn except their clothes, although the pawn tickets analysis (see Appendix) shows that a wide range of other items were pawned, including household items such as tablecloths and cutlery (10.3% of the total items pawned), jewellery including wedding rings (7.5% of the total items pawned) and bedding (3.9% of the total items pawned).

Here is the breakdown of the top ten items pawned at Collier's South Street shop, as shown by the pawn tickets analysis (see Appendix):

1. Trousers	8.8%	6. Face flannels	6.9%
2. Coats	8.4%	7. Shirts	6.9%
3. Boots	7.6%	8. Jackets	5.2%
4. Vests	7.6%	9. Frocks	3.9%
5. Suits	7.4%	10. Gowns	3.4%

It was quite common for people to pawn items on a Monday and redeem them on the following Saturday, after the household's wage earner had been paid; "best" clothes were a good example of this, being worn for church or chapel on the Sunday and pawned again the next day. The drawing opposite depicts Saturday night at the pawnbroker's, and gives a striking impression of how busy pawn shops could be on such nights.

The pawn tickets analysis (see Appendix) helps to put Knowles' figures into perspective, in terms of the amounts Collier lent his customers for the items they pawned. Here is the distribution of these amounts, bearing in mind that some were for multiple items:

- 3.2% from 1d to 11d (0.59p to £6.49)
- 62% from 1s to 4s 11d (£7.15 to £35.09)
- 19% from 5s to 9s 11d (£35.75 to £70.84)
- 6.4% from 10s to 19s 11d (£71.50 to £142.34)
- 1.3% from £1 to £5 10s (£143 to £785.50).

Workers' living conditions

In the second half of the nineteenth century, many Hull workers lived in inadequate, insanitary housing, and in 1849 these conditions caused a cholera

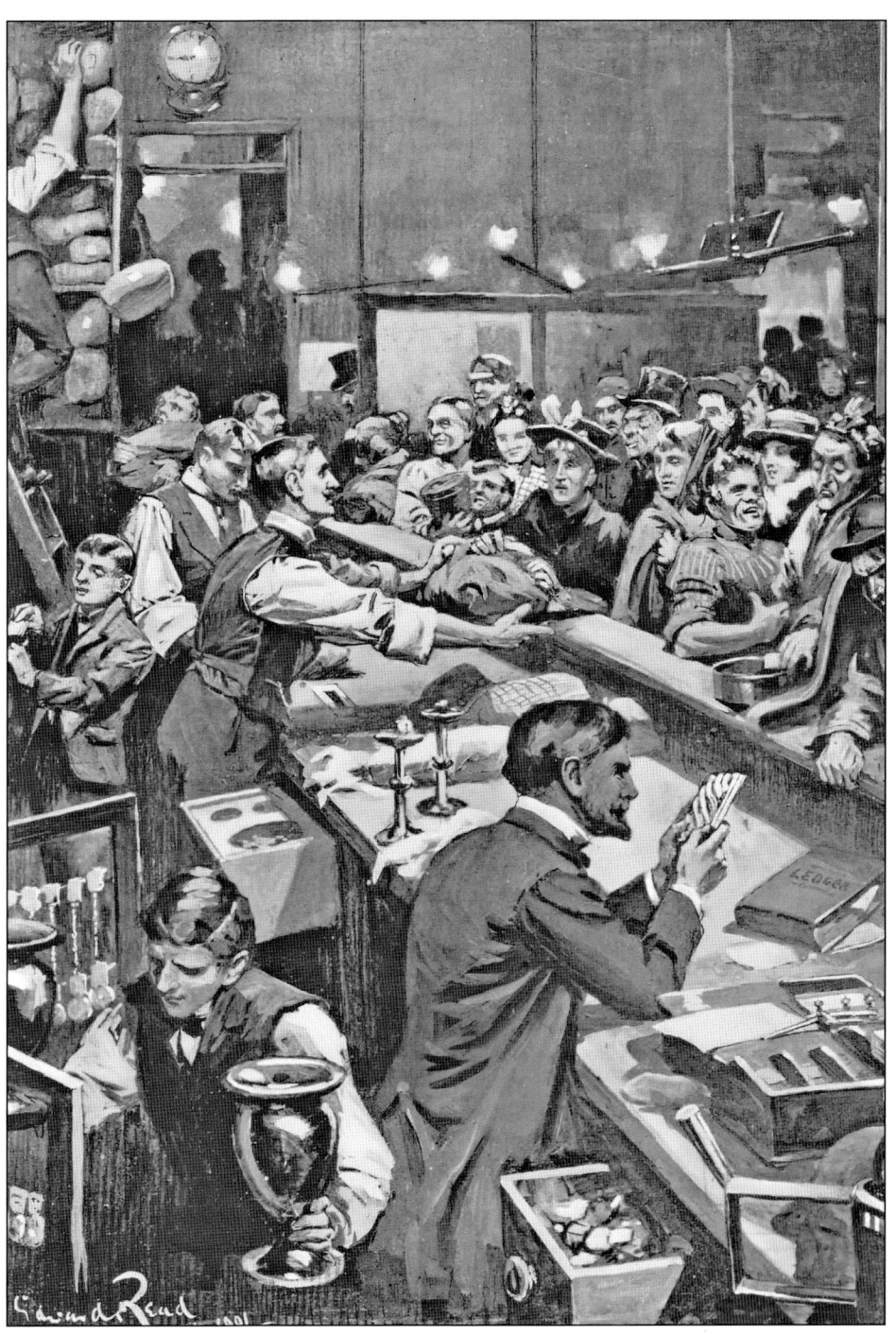

Living London From, 1901. (Higgs, n.d.)

epidemic which killed 1,834 Hull residents (Allison, 1969). The Hull Sanitary Committee reported that housing was poor and overcrowded, the water supply was inadequate, and the sewers emptied into open land drains and then into the River Hull. In the poorer housing with no rear access, the night soil was collected and brought through the house, then taken to "muck garths" and left in large heaps to decompose in the open air amongst the housing. One such muck garth was off Witham in the Drypool area of Hull; the General Board of Health's 1850 report on the aforementioned cholera epidemic has an unpleasantly graphic description of this muck garth:

> On the east side of the town of Hull lies a suburb called Witham in which there is a triangular space of ground bounded by the street called Witham, Great Union Street, and Church Street. This triangle is surrounded by houses, so as to leave an open space in the centre of nearly three acres in extent, about two acres of which is used as a place of deposit for part of the night soil of the town and other manure, which is interspersed in heaps among the houses and close to the doors of the dwellings. These noxious matters are collected by a number of persons who make a trade of accumulating and selling them for agricultural purposes, and they have become so accustomed to live amongst this horrible garbage, that they not only heap it up against the walls and immediately under the windows of their houses but it is stated that they have come to consider the atmosphere of the locality 'rather wholesome and agreeable' than otherwise.
>
> In the month of July 1849 I [the Board of Health Inspector] went over the neighbourhood, and certainly few places have presented more elements of disease and mortality. The surface appeared to be one mass of heaped-up filth. An offensive open ditch ran through the ground, and the whole atmosphere was …polluted to some distance…There is every reason to believe that had these nuisances been summarily dealt with when the first warning was given to the town in September 1848, a great part, if not the whole of the appalling catastrophe which took place might have been averted…The epidemic at last touched the district and committed the most fearful ravages among the people.

The same General Board of Health Report (1850) included the map opposite of the Witham muck garth, which shows clearly how near the housing it was, and also shows the "open offensive drain" (called "ditch" in the quotation above) forming its eastern boundary.

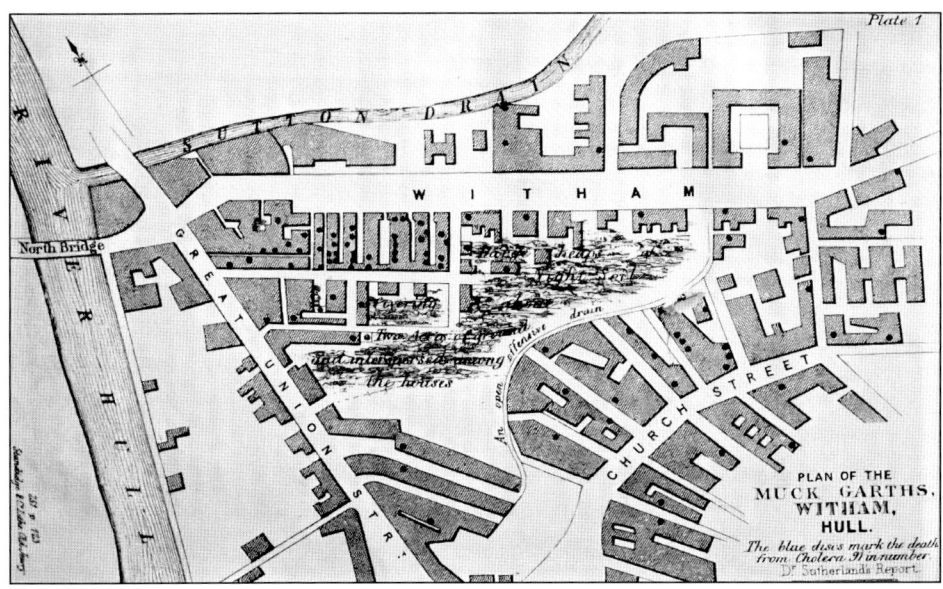

Allison (1969) also describes the 1881 scarlet fever epidemic in Hull, which killed 689 people whose average age was less than five years. In addition, there was a rising number of infant deaths from diarrhoea, which rose from an average of 237 per year in the 1870s to 608 in 1911.

Some of the worst slum housing in Hull was court housing; this was terraced housing in a courtyard behind a main street, which was usually accessed by a narrow archway between two buildings on the front of the main street. The fourth chapter of Gibson (2013) describes this court housing in detail, with accompanying photographs of some of the courts taken by Hull Corporation's Health Department between 1890 and the 1930s, when the Corporation was looking to demolish this housing. Virtually without exception the courts were cramped and overcrowded, with many families living in one up one down houses and quite often in one room in a sub-divided house. In addition, court housing was often back to back with no rear access (see also above). Gibson also points out that unscrupulous landlords only exacerbated these living conditions. The courts themselves were usually deep and narrow, allowing little daylight to come through; sometimes the walls of the houses in the courts were lime or white washed, to try to reflect what little daylight there was. The houses in the court shared one communal cold water tap and communal privies, and there was often an open drain down the middle of the court.

This photograph above (Facebook: Hull the Good Old Days group) is of Whipps Court off South Street, very near Collier's main shop (see below). The communal privies at the end of the court can be seen, and the overcrowding and lack of daylight is clear.

In 1848 the Public Health Act became law, providing a framework for local authorities to improve drainage, remove refuse from the street and from houses, provide clean drinking water and appoint an Officer of Health (UK Parliament, 2022b). However, this was not compulsory and had no real power until Hull Corporation adopted it in 1854 and started to enforce it. Under this act, the byelaws stipulated by the Corporation in relation to new build court housing were that there must be no tunnel (archway) entrances, courts had to be a minimum of 20' wide, each house had to have a backyard, and each house had to be connected to the main drainage system (Gibson, 2013). Sadly this came too late for those living in the existing court housing, much of which was not demolished until well into the 1900s.

The area to the north west of Collier's main shop in South Street was known locally as the West End, i.e. the area bordered by Carr Lane to the south, Spring Street to the west, Spring Bank to the north, and Prospect Street and Chariot Street to the east (see map opposite). The name stems from the fact that at the time, the area was the western part of the city centre.

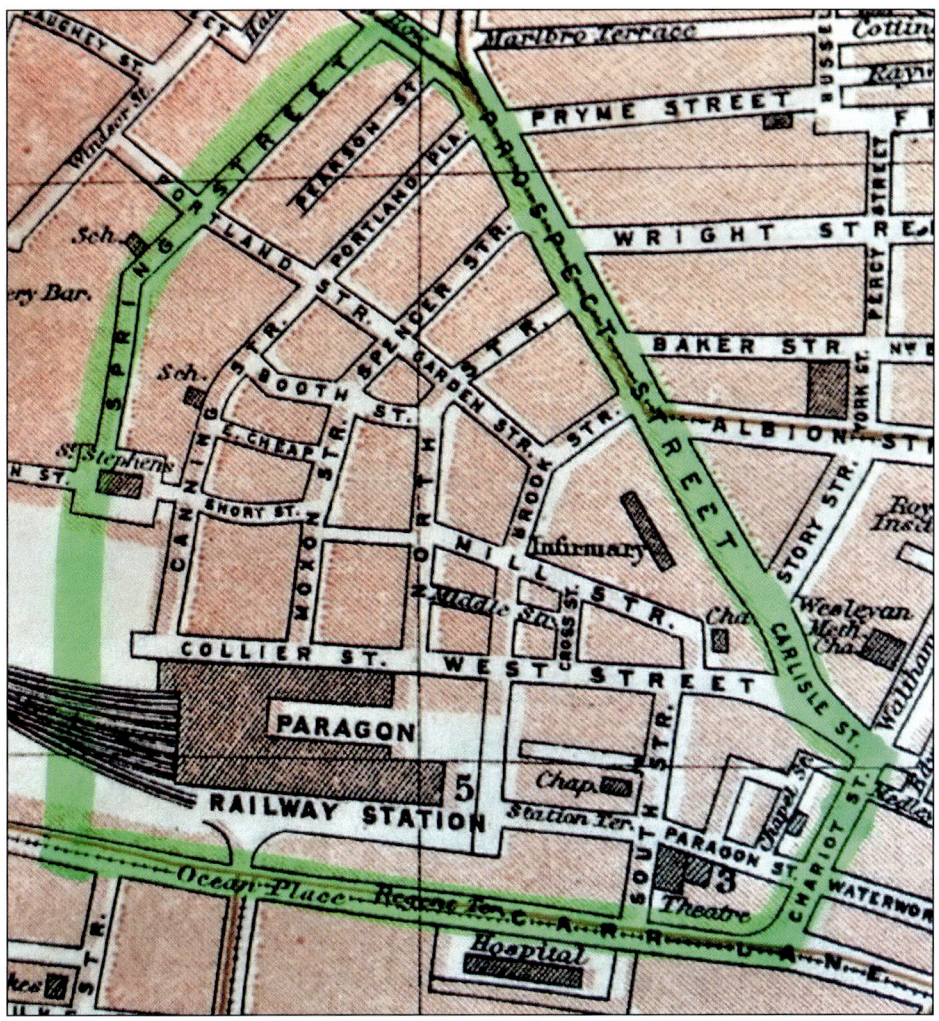

The West End in 1892 (Muirhead, n.d.)

In this area there were many examples of court housing, this also applying to the areas where Collier had his other shops (described in detail later in this book). Much of the West End's slum housing was demolished in the late 1920s for the building of Ferensway, and the occupants rehoused; for example, the author's late mother-in-law's family was rehoused from Spencer Street to Humber Buildings in Madeley Street, off Hessle Road.

The analysis of the 6,871 pawn tickets from Collier's South Street shop (see Appendix), reveals that 74% of the total number of pawn tickets had on them addresses in the West End. In turn, 94% of these were in just three streets, – West Street (immediately adjacent to South Street), Collier Street (an extension of West Street at that time) and South Street itself. These figures emphasise the relatively small catchment area of Collier's South Street shop, and also that most of its customers were more than likely (but not exclusively) from the lower income end of society. The 1896 Ordnance Survey (OS) map below (Carnegie Heritage Centre: maps) shows the part of the West End immediately to the north of Collier's South Street shop, where many examples of court housing can be seen, usually named "square" or "place".

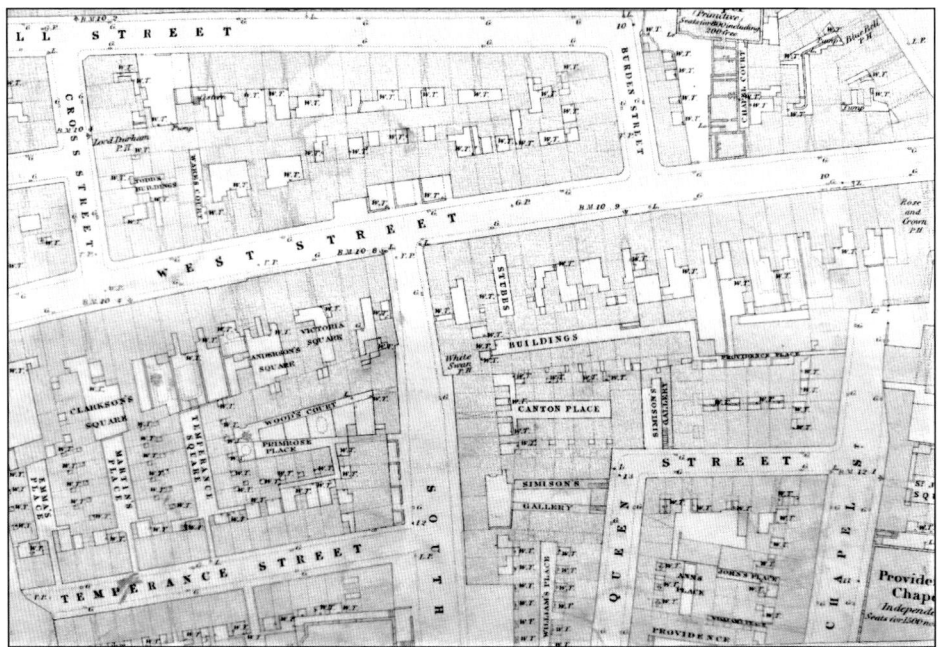

PAWNBROKING NATIONALLY FROM AROUND 1850 TO THE PRESENT DAY

The principles and extent of pawnbroking

Pawnbroking is raising money by taking out a loan against the item(s) being pawned; as long the item(s) remains unredeemed (i.e. in the possession of the pawnbroker), the customer is charged interest on the loan, the rate rising the longer the item(s) remains unredeemed. It is this interest which provided pawnbrokers some of their income. Higgs (n.d.) points out that in Collier's time, pawnbrokers were an integral part of life for families whose breadwinner was working, but poorly paid (see above). The pawn tickets analysis (see Appendix) shows that many families were fairly regular customers at Collier's South Street shop; for example, the Wass family (who lived at various addresses in the West End), used Collier's services 80 times during the eight years from 1888 to 1896. Similarly, the Larkin/Larking family used Collier's services 53 times during the same eight years. Pawnbrokers therefore provided a vital service as an alternative to a bank loan, as few people in the lower income bracket at that time would have had a bank account anyway. It could also be argued that pawning their belongings saved some families from entering the workhouse, a fate which was universally dreaded.

Having said that, it should be acknowledged that not all pawnbrokers' customers were from the working classes; the middle classes (and even the upper classes) who had fallen on hard times also used their services. This is borne out by the pawn tickets analysis (see Appendix) which shows that a small minority of Collier's customers lived not in the West End (see above) but in some of the relatively prosperous areas of the period, such as parts of Beverley Road. One such customer pawned in one visit to Collier's South Street shop, three watches (including a gold one), a brooch and several rings for a total of £5 10s (£786.50), the highest amount of all those on the 6,871 pawn tickets found hidden up the chimney.

Pawnbroking expanded greatly in Victorian times, following the Industrial Revolution and the rise in the urban population, as described above; the National Pawnbrokers Association of the UK (n.d.) states that during Collier's time there were nearly as many pawnbrokers as public houses! Indeed, in response to this, the National Pawnbrokers Association of the UK itself was founded in 1892. Maxcroft Pawnbrokers (2020) emphasise the point about expansion during this period, estimating that in 1750 there were around 750 pawnbrokers in Britain, this number rising to around 4,500 by 1850.

During the interwar years and especially after the Second World War, the importance of pawnbroking waned somewhat, following in particular the aforementioned introduction of the UK's social security system in 1948. However, it is interesting to note that recent times have seen a revival, following the 2008 recession and very recently, the rapidly rising cost of living. Indeed, at the time of writing in 2022, many strikes have already taken place or are scheduled to do so throughout the so called "summer of discontent", mirroring the strikes of 1889 as described above. The National Pawnbrokers Association of the UK (n.d.) estimates that in 2020 there were up to 2,000 pawn shops in the UK, and it is likely that this number has risen since then. Modern pawnbrokers operate using virtually the same principles as during Collier's time, although items pawned tend to be no longer the basics of life such as clothing, rather "luxury" goods such as mobile phones, gold jewellery and cameras; in addition, some pawnbroking is done online.

The pawnbroking legislation in force in the second half of the nineteenth century

The first modern Pawnbrokers Act was enacted in 1800, followed by amendments in 1815, 1840 and 1860 (Wikipedia, 2022), but the act in force during the years of the pawnbrokers tickets hidden up the chimney in Collier's South Street shop (1887 to 1896) was the Pawnbrokers Act 1872 (UK Parliament, 1872). This repealed, altered and consolidated all previous pawnbroking related legislation, and was welcomed by pawnbrokers as it removed some of the previous restrictions on their businesses and also gave them a clearer framework in which to operate. In fact, much of this Act is effectively still in force today, as amended by the 1974 Consumer Credit Act.

There is a link to the full text online of the 1872 Pawnbrokers Act in the list of Sources Used (UK Parliament, 1872), but here is a summary of the main points of the act:

- A pawnbroker's licence would only be granted by a magistrate if the applicant was of good character, as attested to by respectable citizens (as referees).
- The annual tax on pawnbrokers was reduced from £15 (£2,142) to £7 10s (£1,072.50).
- Restrictions on pawnbrokers' hours of trading were abolished.
- The act's schedules specified the details of the documentation and book keeping systems pawnbrokers had to use. Collier's book keeping appears to have fallen short of these standards, an issue which will be discussed later in this book.
- The act applied to every loan made by a pawnbroker, up to but not above £10 (£1,428)
- The amount of interest that could be charged on pawned items was stipulated, being on a rising scale depending on the amount of money

> **A—For Loan of 10s. and under.—The Pawnbroker is entitled to charge:—For this Ticket. One Halfpenny.** For profit on each Two Shillings or part of Two Shillings lent on this pledge for not more than one calendar month, One Halfpenny, and so on at the same rate per calendar month. After the first calendar month any time not exceeding fourteen days will be charged as half a month, and any time exceeding fourteen days and not more than one month will be charged as one month. This pledge must be redeemed within twelve calendar months and seven days from the date of pledging. At the end of that time it becomes the property of the Pawnbroker. If the pledge is destroyed or damaged by fire the Pawnbroker will be bound to pay the value of the pledge after deducting the amount of the loan and profit, such value to be the amount of the loan and profit, and twenty-five per cent. on the amount of the loan. If this ticket is lost, mislaid, or stolen, the pawner should at once apply to the Pawnbroker for a form of declaration to be made before a magistrate or the Pawnbroker will be bound to deliver the pledge to any person who produces this ticket to him and claims to redeem the same.

lent to the customer and the length of time before that customer redeemed their item(s).

- These rates of interest and the terms and conditions of the agreement (in effect, an implied contract) between the pawnbroker and their customer had to be printed on the back of every pawn ticket; the idea of this was to protect both the pawnbroker and the customer (see photograph above, taken by the author, of the reverse of one of Collier's pawn tickets).

  The exception to this was "special contracts" for items pawned for above £2 (£286); in this case, the rates of interest and terms and conditions of the contract had to be printed on the front of a larger pawn ticket, as they are in the photograph on the next page (taken by the author) of one of Collier's special contract tickets.

- Depending on the amount lent to a customer, different rules were laid down for the ownership of the pawned items, as well as either their eventual redemption by the customer or their sale by the pawnbroker.

- Sales by the pawnbroker of unredeemed items pawned for above 10s (£71.50) had to be by public auction. For example, Collier placed an advertisement in the Eastern Morning News of 22nd March 1897 (British Newspaper Archive), for an auction of "valuable forfeited pledges" (i.e. unredeemed items) from his South Street shop (see below), including "First-Class Gold and Silver Watches…Jewellery set with Precious Stones…Diamond Rings…".

> **SPECIAL CONTRACT UNDER ACT OF PARLIAMENT**
>
> Pawned with
> **ROBERT COLLIER, Pawnbroker,**
> 13, South-street (Paragon-street), HULL,
>
> this ___ day of _July_ 188_9_
>
> By _Eliza Ann Nicholson_
> Of _Malton Avenue_
>   _St George's R__
>
> _Gold Lever Watch & Albert_
>
> Money lent on gold and silver.
>
> TERMS OF THE SPECIAL CONTRACT—The Pawnbroker charges—
>
> For this Ticket ___ . Profit at the rate per calendar month of ___
> After the first calendar month, any time not exceeding fourteen days will be charged as half a month, and any time exceeding fourteen days and not more than one month will be charged as one month.
> The charge for storage of this pledge will be ___ per calendar month, or any part of a month, in addition to the charges above-mentioned.
> This pledge is pawned for the period of ___ months (not less than three). After the expiration of that time the pledge may be sold by auction by the Pawnbroker, but it may be redeemed by the pawner at any time before the day of sale. Within three years after sale the pawner may inspect the account of the sale in the Pawnbroker's books on payment of ___ and receive any surplus produced by the sale. But deficit on sale of one pledge may be set off by the Pawnbroker against surplus on another.
> If the pledge is destroyed or damaged by fire the Pawnbroker will be bound to pay the value of the pledge, after deducting the amount of the loan and profit such value to be the amount of the loan and profit and twenty-five per cent. on the amount of the loan, unless otherwise agreed upon by the pawner and Pawnbroker. If this ticket is lost or mislaid the pawner should at once apply to the Pawnbroker for a form of declaration to be made before a magistrate, or the Pawnbroker will be bound to deliver the pledge to any person who produces this ticket to him and claims to redeem the same.
>
> ....Pawnbroker.

- A pawnbroker was not allowed to accept items for pawning from a child under the age of twelve, nor from anyone who was drunk.
- A pawnbroker was also not allowed to accept stolen goods for pawning, although the act safeguarded him or her if they unknowingly did this and/or sold the item(s). Sometimes people attempted to pawn stolen goods at Collier's shops (see below); for example on 29th January 1894, the Hull Daily Mail (British Newspaper Archive) reported that a man had tried to pawn a stolen dungaree jacket at the South Street shop, and was later arrested.

PAWNBROKING IN HULL FROM AROUND 1850 TO THE PRESENT DAY

It goes without saying that during Collier's time, pawnbrokers in Hull would have had to operate under the legislation described above if they wanted to retain their licences. According to the Carnegie Heritage Centre's street directories, the number of pawnbrokers in Hull before, during and after Collier's time was as follows:

YEAR	NO OF PAWNBROKERS	YEAR	NO OF PAWNBROKERS
1851	36	1899	76
1863	52	1907	62
1867	55	1916	49
1875	72	1929	37
1892	72	1933	30
1895	69	1936	23

From this table, it can be seen that the extent of pawnbroking in the city from around 1851 more or less followed the national trends described above, the number of pawnbrokers decreasing from the early twentieth century onwards. The peak years from 1875 to 1907 fall largely during Collier's time, the pawn tickets that were hidden up the South Street chimney being dated from 1887 to 1896, with approximately 96% (6,571 individual tickets) being from the years 1888, 1889 and 1890 (see Appendix).

In 2021 there were around eleven pawnbrokers in Hull (some with more than one branch), all in either the city centre or in areas of relative deprivation, including Hessle Road, Bransholme and Holderness Road (Carnegie Heritage Centre, Hull Yellow Pages), mirroring the revival of pawnbroking nationally, as described above.

ROBERT COLLIER'S PERSONAL LIFE

NOTES
- There are some gaps in this outline of Collier's personal life, because the author was unable to locate any personal records for these "gap years". The same applies to records relating to pawnbroker Elizabeth Dunlin (see below).

- Unless otherwise stated, the family records mentioned in this section are from either the Ancestry or the Find My Past websites.

Collier's personal life from birth in 1842 to 1861 (age 19)

Robert Collier was born in Hull in 1842; his parents were James and Mary Ann, who had been married in 1827. Robert was their fourth child, and his siblings were James (1836-1910), Eliza Harriet (1838-?), Emma (1840-1885), Frances (1844-1914) and Isabella (1847-1917). James Collier was a Humber pilot and in 1848 the family were living at 95 Waverley Street in the Porter Street area of Hull, near Hessle Road. As a Humber pilot, James would have earned a relatively good wage, so it is likely that the family was comfortably off. Indeed, housing in this area was more salubrious than the court housing described above, with larger houses and little or no court housing in the immediate vicinity, as the 1899 OS map below (National Library of Scotland) shows.

In October 1848, Robert's mother Mary Ann died of consumption at the age of 42, when Robert was only six years old and when the ages of his siblings ranged from twelve down to one. The need for a mother for his young children could perhaps explain why James Collier remarried in mid-1850, less than two years after Mary Ann's death; his second wife was also named Mary. In 1851 the family were still living at 95 Waverley Street, but by 1861 they had moved down the road to 58 Waverley Street. As mentioned above, this area was at the time home to those who were comfortably off; the Collier family's neighbours listed in the 1861 Census included another Humber pilot, a master mariner and a brewer.

Collier's personal life from 1861 (age 19) to 1871 (age 29)

NOTE: full details of Collier's pawnbroking business and the premises he owned are in the next main section of this book.

In 1861 Robert Collier was nineteen years old and was listed in the census for that year as a pawnbroker's assistant, but his employer was not stated. It is interesting to note that Collier began his pawnbroking career before he was twenty years old. Also in the household at 58 Waverley Street in 1861 were his stepmother and two unmarried sisters; his father James was not listed on the census record, so it could be that he was on the river when the census was taken, working at his job as Humber pilot. In 1868, when Collier was 26 years old, his father died from paralysis at the age of 60; at the time of his death, James was living at 7 Bank Street off Derringham Street (see also below).

The 1871 Census lists Robert Collier living as a boarder at 1 West Street in the centre of Hull, which as far as the author can ascertain, was at the corner of West Street and Prospect Street (then Carlisle Street – see 1892 map of the West End, above). Collier was single (remaining so throughout his life) and was living in the household of 40 year old widow Elizabeth Dunlin, along with her son, three daughters and a female domestic servant. Dunlin is listed as a pawnbroker and as in the 1861 Census, Collier is listed as a pawnbroker's assistant, so it is very likely that in 1871 he was Dunlin's employee, effectively her apprentice.

Pawnbroker Elizabeth Dunlin (1831 to 1902)

In the light of Collier being employed by pawnbroker Elizabeth Dunlin in 1871, the author has researched Dunlin's life and pawnbroking business, as a comparison with and to add context to those of Collier. The findings of this research will be drawn on in subsequent sections of this book.

Dunlin was born in Hull in 1831, and by 1861 was married to pawnbroker William; at that time they had two daughters and were living at 7 West Street, along with a female domestic servant. William died of consumption in 1869, at the age of 47, and by then the couple had four children, aged from fifteen down to two. This is a similar story to that of the Collier family i.e. the loss of one parent when the children were young, although at that time this situation was probably not unusual.

Dunlin took over her husband's pawnbroking business after he died, and by 1871 the family had moved to 1 West Street, where as described above, Collier lived with them as Dunlin's assistant in her business. The employment of a domestic servant during William Dunlin's time and after he died, indicates that the Dunlins' pawnbroking business was likely to be lucrative. Indeed, this mirrors the later success of Collier's business, and these successes are borne out by further research, detailed later in this book.

Collier's personal life from 1876 (age 34) to 1895 (age 53)

By 1876, at the age of 34, Collier had moved out of 1 West Street to 2 Bank Street, off Derringham Street; it is possible that this was actually 7 Bank Street where his father James was living at the time of his death in 1868 (see above), because in the handwritten censuses of the time, the numbers 2 and 7 could easily be mistaken for each other. Equally, James could have died at 2 Bank Street. By June 1878 at the age of 36, Collier owned his own freehold pawnbrokers shop at 13 South Street (discussed in more detail in the next main section of this book). Collier's ownership of 13 South Street is evidenced in an article in the Hull Daily Mail of 28th June 1878 (British Newspaper Archive), which reported an attempt to pawn a stolen watch there. Incidentally, when Collier realised that the watch was stolen, he kept the suspect in conversation whilst his shop assistant fetched a policeman, effectively performing a citizen's arrest!

The 1881 Census lists Collier as a pawnbroker age 39, living at 13 South Street, presumably above the shop; he may have moved there earlier from Bank Street, as he had bought South Street by 1878. In October 2020, the author visited the South Street premises during their conversion into flats (see above) and the ornate original staircase was still in place (although somewhat dirty due to the building work being carried out), indicating that this was by no means slum housing at that time. Opposite are two photographs of the staircase, taken by the author on this visit.

Living with Collier at 13 South Street were his widowed stepmother Mary (age 79) and a female general domestic servant Charlotte Saville (age 23), the latter confirming that even at this early stage, Collier's pawnbroking business was lucrative enough for him to employ such a servant, as was Elizabeth Dunlin's business (see above). The pawn tickets spreadsheet analysis (see Appendix) of the amounts loaned to Collier's customers is further evidence of the potential profit he was making.

Indeed, the 1881 Census has further evidence of Dunlin's prosperity. At that time, at the age of 50, she was living at Osborne Villa on the north side of Spring Bank, near its junction with Princes Avenue; this was a large three storey terraced house with bay windows, in a then respectable area. Osborne Villas was in the row of houses on the right in the photograph bottom of the previous page (Facebook: Hull Chat Group); these properties still stand today, but with their ground floors converted into shops.

In the 1881 Census there are no employment details for Dunlin, so it is not known whether she remained a pawnbroker or had retired by then. If Dunlin was retired by 1881, it could be that Collier picked up some of her customers, as he had his South Street shop in 1978 if not earlier. This is made more likely by Dunlin's West Street shop being just around the corner from Collier's South Street shop. Also in the Dunlin household in 1881 were her three daughters and one son, all single; there is no servant listed in the census, but it could be that the eldest daughter performed domestic duties, as there is no employment listed for her either.

Returning to Collier, his stepmother Mary died age 82 of bronchitis at 13 South Street in February 1884, so it can probably be assumed that at that time the family were still living above the shop. Various articles in the Hull Daily Mail in 1888 and 1889 (British Newspaper Archive) show that Collier appeared to be a respectable and well known businessman during this period, providing character references to magistrates so that under the 1872 Pawnbrokers Act (see above), prospective pawnbrokers and alehouse owners could obtain their licences.

By March 1890 Collier employed a caretaker at his South Street shop, who is mentioned in a Hull Daily Mail article dated 31st March that year (British Newspaper Archive). The article covered a robbery from the shop, and states that "he [Collier] left his shop in the charge of a caretaker, at about 8pm… About three o'clock the following morning he [Collier] was called up and proceeded to his shop…" It can be assumed from this that Collier was by then no longer living above his South Street shop.

To support this, the 1891 Census shows Collier listed as a 49 year old pawnbroker living at 32 Coltman Street in west Hull, which was then a very respectable area indeed. The house was demolished in 1941 after being bombed during the Second World War, but is in the photograph opposite (Facebook: Hull Chat group), approximately to the right of the lamp post in the far right distance. Also living there in 1891 were a housekeeper and a domestic servant, both single as Collier still was, so he was clearly prosperous.

Another indicator of Collier's prosperity was the expansion of his business into two more shops, one in Dock Street, which Collier had in 1892 (Carnegie Heritage Centre: street directories), and the other in Castle Street, which he had in 1894 (Hull Daily Mail: British Newspaper Archive). There are full details of all Collier's shops in the next main section of this book.

At this time Elizabeth Dunlin also appears to have been prosperous. The 1891 Census shows her to be age 60 and living at 4 Carlton Villas (number 106) in Boulevard in west Hull, at that time another very respectable area; the imposing semi-detached house with its bay window still stands on the western side of Boulevard (see photograph overleaf, taken by the author in November 2020). Even more indicative of her prosperity, Dunlin was described in the census as "living on own means", presumably on the profits made from her pawnbroking business.

In 1895 at the age of 53, Collier was still living at 32 Coltman Street, but only three years later this would change.

Collier's personal life from 1898 (age 57) to his death in 1913 (age 71)

1898 was a landmark year for 56 year old Collier, when he sold his South Street business to Leeds jewellers and pawnbrokers Owen and Robinson Ltd; the Castle Street and Dock Street shops were not included in the sale, as by then Collier had vacated them. There are full details of this sale in the next main section of this book, but suffice to say, it would have made Collier an even wealthier man. This is evidenced by the 1901 Census, which lists Collier (age 59) as a retired pawnbroker, although it is more than likely that he actually retired in 1898 at the age of 56, immediately after the sale of his South Street shop to Owen and Robinson Ltd. 56 was (and still is today) a relatively early retirement age, so clearly Collier was wealthy enough to do this. In 1901 Collier was living at 72 Coltman Street, a larger

property than number 32 where he had moved from, another indication of his increasing wealth. He was still single and also at this address lived his housekeeper, Alice Lowe. Collier was still living there in 1911, and was to remain there until he died in 1913; the apparently loyal Alice was also in the household in 1913. 72 Coltman Street, with its ornately decorated frontage, still stands on the eastern side of Coltman Street, which is now a conservation area (see photographs below, and overleaf, taken by the author in November 2020).

Looking at the 1901 Census, Elizabeth Dunlin (then age 70) also still appears to be wealthy; by then she had moved from Osborne Villa on Spring Bank to Argyle Villa at 270 Northgate in Cottingham. She remained "living on own means", and living with her were two daughters and a son (all still single), one grandson and one granddaughter; also in the household was a domestic servant.

Argyle Villa was at one time owned by the Ringrose family as part of their extensive Cottingham Grange Estate, so it seems possible that Dunlin might have been a tenant of the property, although the author was unable to establish this with any certainty. When the Ringroses sold the house in 1930, it was described as having two sitting rooms and four bedrooms, as well as a kitchen and scullery (Facebook: Cottingham the Good Old Days group). Argyle Villa still stands on the northern side of Northgate (see photograph below, taken by the author in 2020), and is now called Argyle House. On 5th February 1902, Dunlin died at home age 70 of gallstones and cardiac failure, and on 8th February she was interred in the Dunlin family grave in Hull General Cemetery on Spring Bank West, alongside her husband William and several other family members.

Returning to Collier, he died age 71 on 3rd December 1913, and three days later he was interred in his family's grave in Hull General Cemetery on Spring Bank West, alongside his father, mother, stepmother, and nephew. Overleaf is the monumental inscription with further details of those in the grave, which no longer has a headstone.

Collier's will and the estate he left are covered in a later section of this book, as are those of Elizabeth Dunlin.

In memory of/MARY ANN/wife of/JAMES COLLIER/(Humber Pilot)/who died Oct 30th 1848/aged 42 years/Also/the above named/JAMES COLLIER/who died March 9th 1868/ aged 60 years/Also/JAMES COLLIER GILLETT/grandson of the above/born April 20th 1872/died June 22nd 1873/Also MARY/second wife of the above named/JAMES COLLIER/ who died Feb 6th 1884/aged 82 years/How sweet the memory of her life/Also ROBERT/ youngest son of the above named/JAMES COLLIER/who died Dec 3rd 1913/in his 72nd year/He giveth his beloved sleep.   C31/3865G

BR 1848 Nov 2	Mary Ann Collier, 95 Waverley St. 42 Consumption.	
1868 Mar 13	James Collier, Humber Pilot, 7 Bank St. 60 Paralysis. Informt: Robert Collier.	
1873 Jun 25	James Collier Gillett, s of Edward Gillett, Grocer, 11 Lock St. 1yr & 2mons. Measles.	
1884 Feb 9	Mary Collier, widow, 13 South St. 82 Bronchitis	
1913 Dec 6	Robert Collier, 72 Coltman St. 71	

COLLIER'S BUSINESS CAREER

NOTES

- There are some gaps in this outline of Collier's business life, because the author was unable to locate any records for these "gap years"
- Unless otherwise stated, the family records mentioned in this section are from either the Ancestry or Find My Past websites.

As mentioned in the section above about his personal life, Collier had three shops in the centre of Hull: 13 South Street, 43 Dock Street and 15 Castle Street. This section will look at each of Collier's shops in turn and at Collier's business career in general, including the sale of his business to Owen and Robinson Ltd in 1898. There will also be a comparison of Collier's business and properties with those of Kirk and Co Ltd, another pawnbroking business bought by Owen and Robinson Ltd in 1898.

Collier's shop at 13 South Street

In 1876, just prior to Collier's purchase of 13 South Street, it had been occupied by a Miss Foreman, who was a teacher of music and singing (Carnegie Heritage Centre: street directories), so it could be that Miss Foreman sold the premises to Collier, assuming she owned the freehold; if she was a tenant, the building's owner would have sold it to Collier.

13 South Street was Collier's main shop, where the 6,871 pawn tickets were found hidden up the chimney (see above). As shown in blue in the 1891 OS map below (Carnegie Heritage Centre: maps), the shop was on the eastern side of South Street, adjacent to and south of the Waverley Hotel (now the Masters Bar).

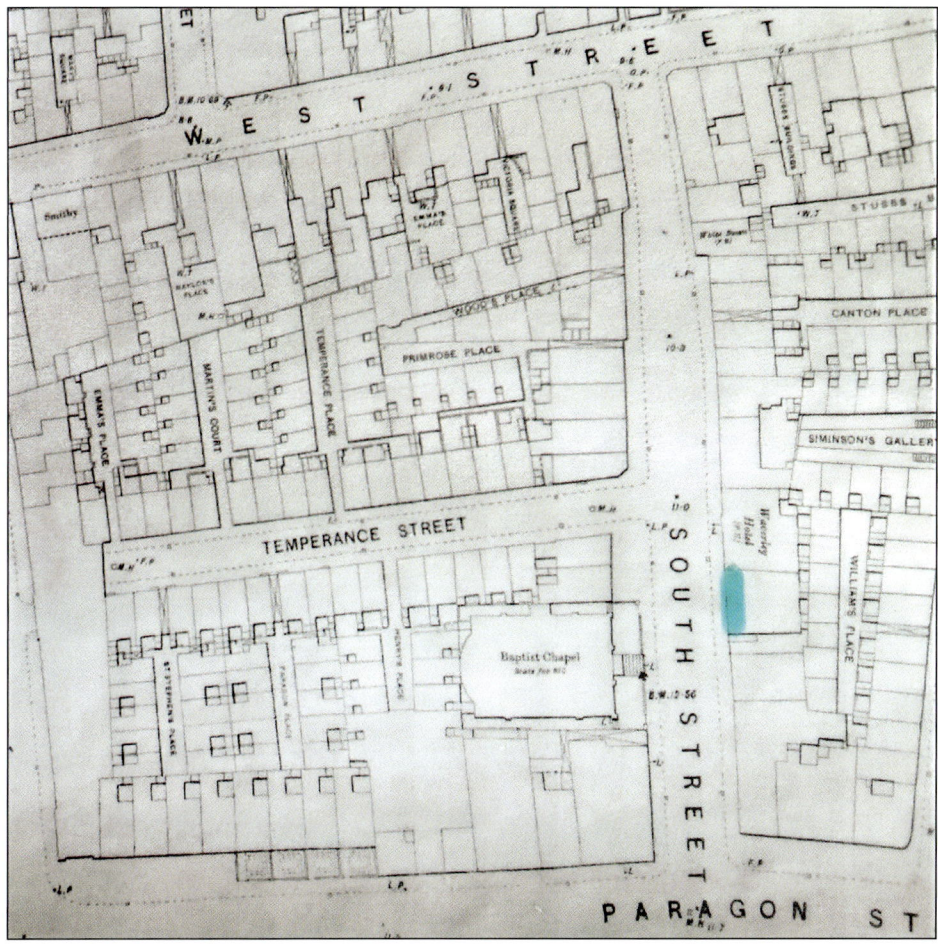

When Collier acquired 13 South Street around 1878, Jameson Street was not yet built, but when it was (in 1903, roughly along the line of Temperance Street), the Waverley Hotel became a corner property at the south east junction of Jameson Street and South Street. South Street was then renumbered, and Collier's shop became numbers 36 to 38, as it remains today.

Gibson (2008) describes how South Street was first laid out around 1802, making Collier's premises amongst the earliest surviving buildings in this area of the city centre. As described above, the shop was in the south east corner of the West End, an area of slum housing, guaranteeing Collier plenty of customers; indeed, in June 1878 business was brisk enough for Collier to employ an assistant, who as the Hull Daily Mail (British Newspaper Archive) reported, helped him when a customer attempted to pawn a stolen watch.

The South Street premises had three storeys and Collier owned the whole building freehold, the family living on the upper floors above the shop until around 1890 (see above). In the 1920s photograph below (Gibson, 2008) of South Street looking north, Jameson Street is at the far left, and the tall building on the corner is the Waverley Hotel, with Collier's former premises immediately adjacent to it.

The Hull Daily Mail (British Newspaper Archive) reported on several thefts from the South Street shop. For example, in March 1890, Collier sued a basket maker of Oxford Street in Hull for breaking and entering the shop and stealing "a silver bracelet, a silver locket and chain, a number of five-shilling pieces, and other articles…" which were worth about £30 (£4,290). The Hull Daily Mail stated that the accused had taken down some of the shutters so that he could access these items, which were displayed in the window; it is interesting to note that not only was Collier's shop vulnerable, with its high value items highly visible in the window, but also that the security shutters which many of today's shops have are nothing new!

Another example of a theft from the South Street shop was reported in the Hull Daily Mail (British Newspaper Archive) on 20th December 1895, by a youth who was employed by Collier in his warehouse. He stole a diamond ring worth £6 10s (£929.50) and was sentenced to 30 days imprisonment.

The sale of Collier's shop at 13 South Street to Owen and Robinson Ltd

As mentioned above, in 1898 Collier sold his South Street shop to new company Owen and Robinson Ltd who were based in Leeds, and at the same time he bought shares in the company, which is discussed in more detail below; this is further evidence of his wealth at this time. The prospectus for this new company was published in the Hull Daily Mail (British Newspaper Archive) on 27th June 1898; it announced the formation of the new company that would amalgamate "the well-known and old-established businesses [in Leeds] of Diamond Merchants, English Watchmakers, Jewellers, General Salesmen and Pawnbrokers" which belonged to William Owen and Benjamin Robinson. Interestingly, one of the directors of Owen and Robinson Ltd was Edward Harland of The Sycamores in Cottingham; his father, also Edward, founded Harland Printers in 1832, and from 1875 the younger Edward ran the company, which still exists today.

The new company also acquired two other businesses, which were: Kirk and Co Ltd, with shops in Leeds and at 29 Grimsby Lane in Hull (more about this below), and Thomas Hammond's Leeds business and premises. All the premises acquired by Owen and Robinson Ltd were freehold, and the company also acquired several other freehold properties including many in Leeds, and in Hull, 54 Paragon Street plus four dwelling houses in Grimsby Lane; all these Hull properties were tenanted. The Grimsby Lane houses and 54 Paragon Street were amongst the properties that were then not being used by Owen and Robinson Ltd, but as the prospectus stated "are being acquired by the Company with a view to utilising them as required for further extensions and other purposes in connection with the Company's business".

Owen and Robinson Ltd moved into 13 South Street soon after they bought it from Collier, and remained there for many years (Carnegie Heritage Centre: street directories); the author remembers shopping there in the 1950s and 1960s. In the 1930s they also had a shop at 11/13 Cleveland Street in Hull near The Groves, an area of slum housing in the industrial area west of the River Hull; like Collier and Dunlin, such an area guaranteed the company plenty of customers. The building was eventually demolished and the site is now occupied by Spiders night club. In addition, Owen and Robinson Ltd owned 13 Holderness Road in Hull from around 1907 to at least 1936 (Carnegie Heritage Centre: street directories); the author has been unable to establish whether the company operated from there or whether it was tenanted. The building still stands on the northern side of Holderness Road, just east of its junction with Dansom Lane.

As mentioned above, Owen and Robinson Ltd also bought 54 Paragon Street in 1898; this was at the south eastern junction of South Street and Paragon Street, and was eventually renumbered to 78, as it remains today. The company owned this property until at least 1933, and let it to various tenants, including George Evans and Sons, rope and twine makers (Carnegie Heritage Centre: street directories). Evans' large premises can be seen in the 1920s photograph of South Street, above.

Returning to the 1898 prospectus, it went on to report the valuations done on all these properties and businesses, for the purpose of the formation of the new limited company. Unfortunately, there were no valuations for the individual properties, nor for their fixtures, fittings and stock (with the exception of 29 Grimsby Lane – see below), so it is impossible to know how much Collier's property and business were worth at that time, and therefore impossible to estimate how much money he received from the sale of 13 South Street.

Also in the prospectus were estimates of the profits of each of the businesses to be acquired by Owen and Robinson Ltd. The prospectus stated that:

> No proper system of book-keeping has been kept in connection with the businesses to be acquired from Messrs Collier and Hammond, but from such details as have been kept, and a careful examination of the materials available, we have satisfied ourselves that it is reasonable to anticipate therefrom a profit [annually] of £750 0s 0d [£107,250].

However, because this estimate was for both Collier's and Hammond's businesses, there is no way of knowing what proportion was Collier's profits. Another important point here in terms of why the 6,871 pawn tickets were hidden up the chimney at 13 South Street, is the fact that Collier's book keeping was not up to standard. This and other possible explanations for the pawn tickets being hidden are discussed later in this book.

Kirk and Co Ltd

At this point it is interesting to look at the business and property of Kirk and Co Ltd, also sold to Owen and Robinson Ltd in 1898, as a comparison with those of Collier and Elizabeth Dunlin. At that time the company had two shops in Leeds as well as the shop at 29 Grimsby Lane in Hull. In this way the company was comparable to that of Collier who at one time had three shops, although these were all in Hull with none in Leeds; Dunlin on the other hand, only had her West Street shop, as described above. The Kirk family were long established not only as pawnbrokers, but also as notable clock and watch makers (a broader business than either Collier's or Dunlin's). Their clocks are apparently still collectable, for example in 2011 one of Thomas Kirk's bracket clocks sold for £2,250 at auction (LotSearch, n.d.)

One branch of the family occupied 29 Grimsby Lane from 1842 (or possibly earlier) until the business was sold to Owen and Robinson Ltd in 1898 (Carnegie Heritage Centre: street directories). During these 56 years, the business is variously described in street directories as "pawnbroker and watch maker", pawnbroker and jeweller" and "pawnbroker and silversmith". In 1892, the family also had a jeweller's shop at 7 Whitefriargate in Hull (Carnegie Heritage Centre: street directories).

It seems probable that Kirk and Co Ltd owned the freehold of the four tenanted houses in Grimsby Lane which were also sold to Owen and Robinson Ltd in 1898; at the time of his death, Collier too owned several houses (there is more detail about these below). This is another similarity between these pawnbrokers, and also another indication of their wealth, as they could afford to buy the houses in the first place, and then benefitted from the rent paid by their tenants. The estimate of Kirk and Co Ltd's profits in the Owen and Robinson Ltd's prospectus of 1898 is another wealth indicator; the company's profits were an average of £2,007 5s 1d (£287,037.34) per year, albeit from three shops, not just from 29 Grimsby Lane. Pawnbroking was certainly a lucrative business to be in, or at least it appeared to be for Collier, Dunlin and Kirk!

Grimsby Lane was a narrow twisting alleyway, running between High Street and Market Place in Hull's Old Town. As with the areas around Collier's and Dunlin's shops, the area around Grimsby Lane comprised largely of overcrowded, insanitary properties, including some court housing (as described above), giving Kirk and Co Ltd plenty of customers. The 1891 OS map overleaf above (National Library of Scotland Maps) shows this clearly, as does the photograph on page 43, dated around 1912 (Gibson, 2008). What can also be seen from the map is that along the short length of Grimsby Lane, there were four public houses!

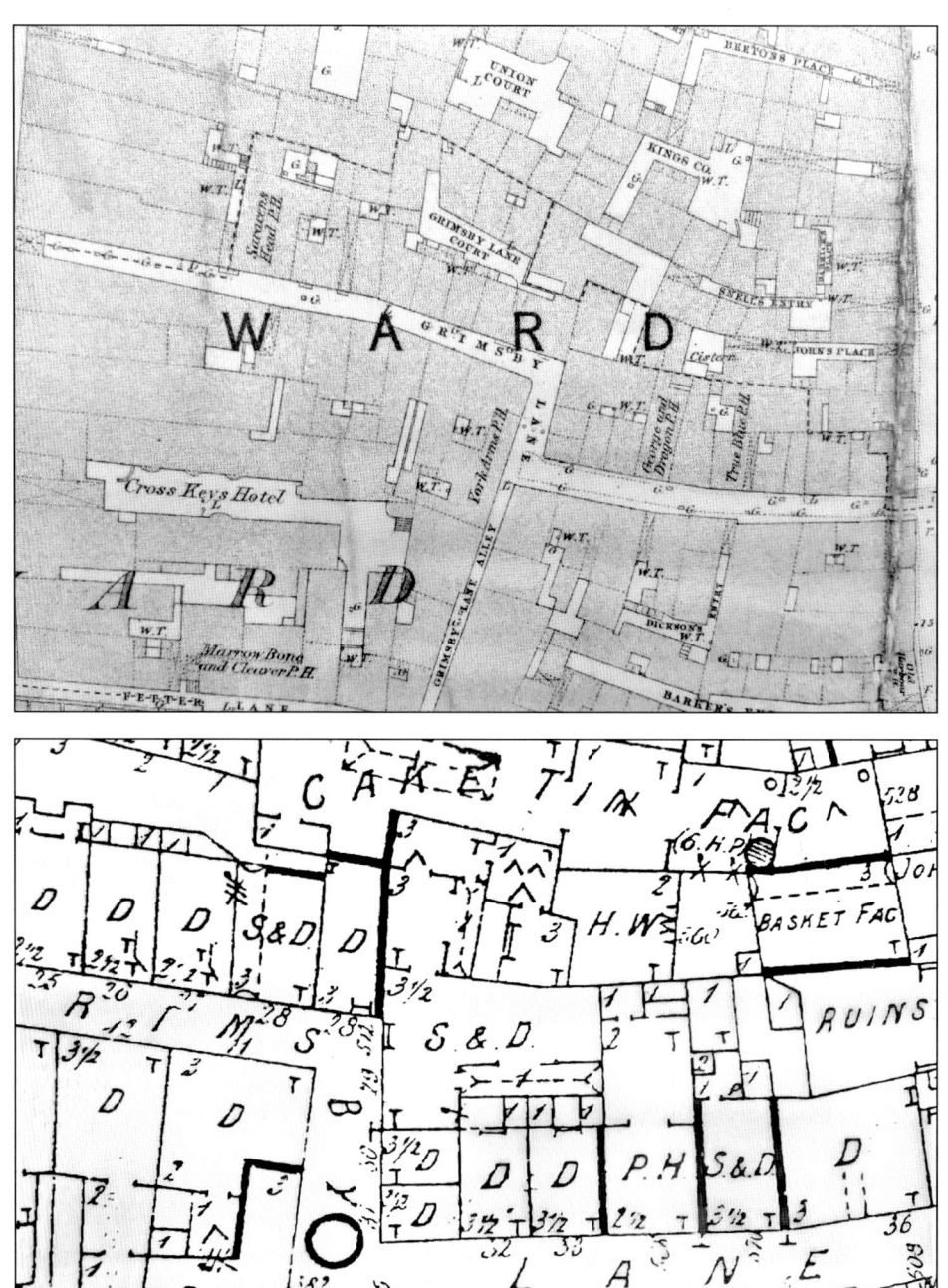

The 1886 Goad's insurance map at the bottom of page 42 (Carnegie Heritage Centre: maps), shows Kirk and Co Ltd's premises at 29 Grimsby Lane; they are the large property in the middle of the map, marked S. & D. i.e. shop and dwelling. These premises were larger than many around them, presumably because there

was a more spacious living area than the norm in the area, and most likely an adjacent warehouse.

As with 13 South Street, Owen and Robinson Ltd moved into 28 Grimsby Lane soon after they bought it in 1898, and remained there until at least 1916 (Carnegie Heritage Centre: street directories). All the area was demolished for redevelopment soon after the Second World War, but the High Street entrance to Grimsby Lane, as well as the entrances to several other long gone alleyways and courts, is still commemorated (see photograph above, taken by the author in January 2021).

Collier's shop at 43 Dock Street

Once Collier's South Street shop was fully established he expanded his business into two additional premises in Hull, the first being 43 Dock Street, which ran along the northern side of Queens Dock (now Queens Gardens). This shop was

immediately east of the entrance to Wilson's Court, and is marked in green on the 1853 OS map above (Carnegie Heritage Centre: maps).

As with the premises of all the pawnbrokers covered in this book, much of the immediate area around Dock Street was slum housing, guaranteeing plenty of customers. One difference however, is that to the north of Dock Street was Charlotte Street (now George Street); this was part of Hull's Georgian New Town, an area of large properties built to house those who had become wealthy as Hull's industries developed (as described above). It is therefore probable that the customers using Collier's Dock Street shop came from a relatively small catchment area compared with those using his South Street shop, which had a larger area of slum housing around it. In addition, the Dock Street shop may well have been used by workers at the adjacent Queens Dock.

Collier occupied 43 Dock Street (see photograph below) from around 1892 to at least 1896 (Carnegie Heritage Centre: street directories), during the period when the number of pawnbrokers in Hull was at its peak, as shown in the table above. The shop was not included in the sale of Collier's business to Owen and Robinson Ltd in 1898 (see above), so it could be that Collier was the tenant not the owner of 43 Dock Street.

Prior to Collier moving in, 43 Dock Street had been occupied since 1876 by another pawnbroker, Mrs Eliza Davison, so presumably Collier would have inherited an established customer base. Furthermore, when Collier moved out of 43 Dock Street Davison again occupied the premises, still operating there as a pawnbroker until at least 1907 (Carnegie Heritage Centre: street directories).

In the photograph above, enlarged from the one from page 46, the name Davison above the shop window can just about be made out; it looks as though it has either been imposed on top of other names, covered by other names, or both, given that Davison occupied the shop before and after Collier's occupancy. The pawnbroker part of the name board is much clearer.

Collier placed six small advertisements in the Hull Daily Mail of 21 December 1894 (British Newspaper Archive) offering items for sale at his Dock Street shop, possibly aiming at the Christmas market of that year but also, as one advertisement says "on account of year-end Stocktaking"; similarly, another advertisement offered a "First-Class Pianoforte, by eminent London maker", on account of "room wanted". The advertisements cover an eclectic mix of items, including watches, violins, two bicycles, a "Splendid Concert Banjo" and a "Mechanical Working Model, six Working Figures…suit shop keeper for window". A bicycle with pneumatic tyres was offered as a "rare bargain" for £7 10s (£1,072.50), whilst the banjo was for sale for 35s (£250.25).

Like 13 South Street (see above), 43 Dock Street was also subject to thefts from time to time. Two by the same person were reported in the Hull Daily Mail on 29th

July 1896 (British Newspaper Archive), when a pair of trousers was taken from the shop door, followed by a shirt the next day. The man was found guilty and sent to prison for six weeks.

43 Dock Street and its surrounding premises were demolished after the Second World War to make way for the Central Police Station and the George Street car park (Gibson, 2008).

Collier's shop at 15 Castle Street

Collier's third shop was at 15 Castle Street in Hull, which he occupied for at least two years, in 1894 and 1895 (Carnegie Heritage Centre: street directories); as with both his other shops, this was during the period when the number of pawnbrokers in Hull was at its peak, as shown in the table above. 15 Castle Street was a lock up shop and was not included in the sale of Collier's business to Owen and Robinson Ltd in 1898 (see above), so as with 43 Dock Street, it seems that Collier was the tenant not the owner of the premises.

15 Castle Street was near the eastern junction of Castle Street with Waterhouse Lane in the centre of Hull, to the west of the well-known Earl Grey public house. Both can be seen below in a relatively recent photograph (Facebook: Hull the Good Old Days group); the Earl Grey is on the far right and the boarded up 15 Castle Street is immediately to the right of the corner premises, Castle Buildings.

The 1907 OS map opposite (National Library of Scotland Maps) shows 15 Castle Street, marked in green. In terms of customers using this shop, there appears

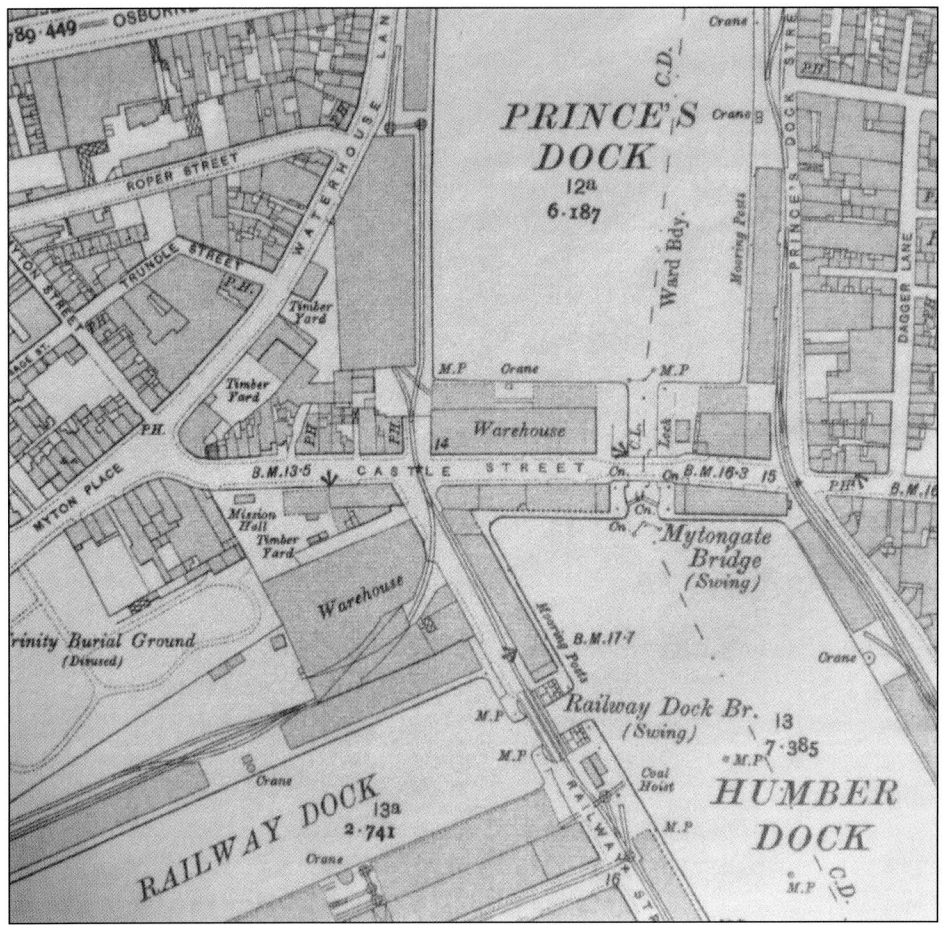

to some court housing in this area and also some terraced housing, neither of which would be likely to house the comfortably off. The Castle Street shop was also adjacent to three of Hull's docks, and it could well be that the dock workers generated some business for Collier there.

As with his other two shops, 15 Castle Street appears to have been vulnerable to theft. An article in the Hull Daily Mail on 31st August 1894 (British Newspaper Archive) details the appearance at the Hull Police Court of a couple who broke into the shop and stole "two plated tea and coffee services, three pairs of opera glasses, one pair of marine glasses, a shawl, bedtick [mattress] and various other articles". It was estimated that the stolen goods were worth between £40 (£5,720) and £50 (£7,150). The couple were sent to trial at the Sessions (the highest criminal court in a district, which tried those accused of serious offences).

15 Castle Street was demolished as part of the wholesale redevelopment of the area from the mid/late 1980s onwards, for the building of the Princes Quay Shopping Centre and the widening of Castle Street (the A63).

COLLIER'S WILL AND THE ESTATE HE LEFT

As outlined above, Collier died on 3rd December 1913. This section will look at the probate granted after his death together with his estate and will, and will also compare them to those of pawnbroker Elizabeth Dunlin. Unless otherwise stated, the details of the wills discussed in this section were obtained from the National Probate Registry (see Sources Used).

NOTE: where necessary in the quotations used in this section, the author has inserted commas to improve their readability.

Collier's will and estate

Collier's probate was granted on 23rd January 1914 to the two executors named in his will i.e. Henry Tom Greaves paint and colour merchant of 95 Gladstone Street in Hull (who was married to Collier's niece), and John Murray (Collier's brother-in-law) commercial traveller of 11 Trinity Square, Anlaby Road in Hull. The gross value of Collier's estate was £4,297 17s 4d (£614,594.91), clearly attesting to the considerable wealth he had amassed during his career as a pawnbroker.

Collier's original will was drawn up in March 1910, but he added a codicil in October 1913, less than two months before he died. The witnesses to the original will were William Henry Boddy (gentleman) of 144 Coltman Street and John Henry Bradley (fish salesman) of 127 Coltman Street; their occupations arguably indicate that Collier was part of the Coltman Street community of comfortably off individuals and families living in large houses such as Collier's (described above). The witnesses to the codicil were G.R. Scorrer and Harriet Scorrer of 141 Coltman Street, who it appears were also part of that community. It is interesting to note that in both his original will and the codicil to it, Collier is referred to as a "gentleman"; he had certainly made a fortune from his pawnbroking business, and had gone up in the world!

Although Collier remained single all his life, the marriages of his five siblings produced a number of nieces and nephews who were recognised in his will, as were his only two surviving siblings (the youngest of the family), Frances Murray, who died in 1914, and Isabella Gillett, who died in 1917. There were also bequests to some of Collier's friends and those who had served him in various ways during his life. These bequests are further evidence of Collier's wealth, including his astuteness in buying items of some quality for his house, as well as his willingness to invest in housing and shares.

The items that Collier bequeathed to his nieces, nephews and friends in his original will included:

> …my gold watch with the gold chain…my silver plated salver, silver teapot, silver cream jug, silver sugar basin and my silver rat tailed sugar tongs…my pianoforte by Collard and Collard [the largest and most notable United Kingdom piano manufacturers in the 1800s]…my single stone diamond ring…my Shamrock diamond pin…my horseshoe diamond pin…my Chippendale chair…

Another bequest of specific items in Collier's original will was to "my old friend Henry Best" who could choose books from Collier's library. In addition, there was a bequest to Alice Lowe, Collier's housekeeper for over ten years, of "my opal and pearl bracelet and also a legacy of five pounds [£714]". In the codicil to his original will, Collier bequeathed further items to two nieces and a nephew, including "my two oval prints supposed to be by Hogarth" and "my Royal Worcester tea and coffee service".

As mentioned above, Collier invested in the stock market, owning two separate sets of shares which he bequeathed in his original will. One set of shares was in the Hull and Barnsley Railway (built between 1880 and 1885), which he left to a niece. Interestingly, the other set of shares was in Owen and Robinson Ltd, the company Collier sold his business to in 1898 (see above). He had £1,000 (£143,000) invested in the company, of which £800 (£114,400) belonged to the two trustees of the post nuptial settlement of his sister Isabelle Gillett. Collier therefore decreed that these shares should be cashed in and £800 (£114,400) of the proceeds be paid to the two trustees.

By far the biggest beneficiaries of Collier's original will were his two surviving siblings Frances Murray and Isabella Gillett (see above). As well as his house at 72 Coltman Street, it can be seen in his will that Collier owned a further twelve houses, six in Alliance Avenue off Anlaby Road in west Hull, and six in Victor Street off Holderness Road in east Hull, a further indication of his substantial wealth. Frances Murray inherited the Alliance Avenue houses and Isabella Gillett inherited those in Victor Street. Furthermore, each of the two sisters also inherited half of the residue of Collier's estate which was left after the aforementioned bequests, on condition that they paid off any remaining mortgages of the above houses, "my object being to provide a permanent investment with the largest possible income for my said sisters". It can probably be assumed that these houses were tenanted, so the two sisters would be assured in the future of regular incomes from the rents for the houses, as well as being wealthy in their own right.

As for Collier's 72 Coltman Street house, in his original will this was to be sold at auction, together with the contents remaining after all other bequests, the proceeds becoming part of his residual estate which was left to his two sisters (see above). However, the codicil to Collier's will altered this; in it, he bequeathed the house to his painter and decorator nephew:

> …in acknowledgement for services rendered by him to me and by way of remuneration and in satisfaction of any claim he may have against me or my estate for work done for me at my various properties.

Why Collier changed his will in this way may never be known, but suffice to say, the inheritance of his large Coltman Street house would have made his nephew a wealthy man, albeit mostly in bricks and mortar.

As decreed in Collier's will, his executors sold the remaining contents of his Coltman Street house at auction, the proceeds being added to his estate. In several issues of the Hull Daily Mail (British Newspaper Archive) in March 1914, there are advertisements for two auctions. The smaller and more portable items were sold on 24th March at the auction rooms of Messrs N.E. Easton and Son, in Bowlalley Lane in Hull's Old Town; they were described in the advertisement as "a valuable collection of old china, cut glass, silver…pictures, old engravings and prints…jewellery…". The larger items of furniture were sold on 25th March by the same auctioneers at Collier's 72 Coltman Street house; the items were described as "excellent furniture" and included "mahogany chests [of] drawers, toilet tables, bookcases…walnut drawing room chairs, hall stand and chairs…clocks, carpets…"

The details of Collier's will reveal above all else the extent of his considerable wealth at the time of his death, which as described above, increased throughout his pawnbroking career as his business grew, and then increased further when that business was sold to Owen and Robinson Ltd in 1898. It must be acknowledged that some of Collier's wealth may have come from an inheritance from his parents, but whatever estate they left would presumably have been split between the six siblings, so their inheritances may well not have been substantial.

Elizabeth Dunlin's will and estate

As outlined above, Elizabeth Dunlin died on 5th February 1902, although on the probate notice attached to her will, it says that she died on 6th February. Her probate took nearly a year to come through (much longer than Collier's did), and was granted in London on 31st December 1902 to Dunlin's nephew and solicitor's managing clerk Richard Hoodlass Rowson, of 164 Spring Bank in Hull. This house still stands as a substantial three storey terraced villa, and is not very far from Osborne Villa on Spring Bank, where Dunlin had lived at one time (see above).

Rowson was the sole executor of Dunlin's will, whereas Collier appointed two executors. The gross value of Dunlin's estate was £832 15s 7d (£119,087.38), considerably less than Collier's although still substantial; the reasons for this cannot be established with certainty, but it could be that as Dunlin had only one pawnbroking shop as opposed to Collier's three, she made less profit. Also, unlike Collier, Dunlin had been married and had four children, three of whom were still single and living with their mother at the time of her death, so much of her money would have been spent on bringing up the children and perhaps supporting them in their adult life.

Dunlin's will was drawn up on 13th March 1901. The witnesses were Frederick Cappleman and Albert V. Bonner, both clerks to Jackson and Son Solicitors of Hull. The will was shorter than Collier's, and started with a bequest to the aforementioned Rowson of £50 (£7,150) "as an acknowledgement for the trouble he may have in the execution of the trusts in this my will", an interesting statement indeed (there is more detail of these trusts below). In addition, there was a further bequest of £50 (£7,150) to Rowson out of Dunlin's estate.

Dunlin's will was shorter than Collier's, largely because there were only two bequests of specific items owned by Dunlin, whereas Collier made many. Also, Collier owned several properties, whereas Dunlin apparently did not. She left all her silver to her son Frederick, and all her "household furniture, linens, book and pictures" to Frederick and her daughters Alice Maud and Louise Dunlin, "as tenants in common", presumably of Argyle Villa in Cottingham, as these were the three single children who were living there with Dunlin at the time of her death. Also in her will, Dunlin forgave her daughter Ada Hannah Wray and her husband any arrears in the interest they were paying to her on a loan to them of £600 (£85,800). It may never be known what this loan was for, but it was a substantial amount, showing that although Dunlin was not as wealthy as Collier at the time of her death, she was nevertheless very comfortably off.

The remainder of Dunlin's will outlined the trusts which her executor Rowson was designated to administer, and here it becomes clearer why Dunlin thought that this might be a difficult task for him, as mentioned above. She bequeathed the whole of the remainder of her estate (once the bequests detailed above had been fulfilled) to Rowson, and in turn to "his heirs, executors, administrators and assigns". Once the estate had been converted to money, Rowson and his heirs were to hold this money in trust, investing up to two thirds of it in his name, for example in stocks and public funds. Dunlin also stipulated in her will that Rowson could vary these investments "from time to time", and that the income from them was also to come directly into funds held by the trust.

Dunlin then bequeathed this investment income (via the trust administered by Rowson) to her daughter Ada Hannah Wray during her life; in turn, after Ada's death, this money was to be returned to the trust and out of it, Dunlin's grandson Alfred Ernest Wray (Ada's son) was to inherit £100 (£14,300). As for the remainder of Dunlin's estate and investments, Rowson was instructed to "pay and divide the same equally…between my children…Frederick William Dunlin and Clara Taylor [it is unclear who Clara was], Alice Maud Dunlin and Louisa Dunlin." In other words, Rowson was Dunlin's heir, as opposed to her children who would have been her natural heirs, and as such Rowson would keep control of Dunlin's estate, holding it in trust, investing it as he saw fit, and allocating it to members of Dunlin's family as per her instructions.

The furore that this would have caused amongst Dunlin's children can only be imagined; what is almost certain is that at that time, Rowson was in an unenviable position! However, all this begs the question of why Dunlin did not leave her estate directly to her children, preferring it to be administered and controlled by Rowson. There could be many reasons for this stipulation; for example, Dunlin apparently wanted all her children to inherit some of her estate, but not equally. Perhaps she did not trust her children to share out her estate in this way, or thought that one or more of them might squander their share if they were left in control.

From Dunlin's will it can be seen that although she was not as wealthy at the time of her death as Collier was when he died, she was still very comfortably off, this being yet more evidence of the profitability of pawnbroking in the second half of the nineteenth century.

THE UNSOLVED MYSTERY: WHY WERE 6,871 PAWN TICKETS HIDDEN UP THE CHIMNEY IN COLLIER'S SOUTH STREET PREMISES?

This book began with a remarkable discovery and ends with the still unsolved mystery of why 6,871 pawn tickets, all around 130 years old and belonging to pawnbroker Robert Collier, were found hidden (apparently deliberately) as far up the chimney as possible in his South Street premises. The reason(s) will probably never be known, but nevertheless it is worth discussing some possible explanations, particularly in the light of how well regarded Collier appeared to be as both a person and as a businessman.

Collier as a person and a businessman

From the analysis above of Collier's personal and business life, it can be seen that:

- His father was a Humber pilot, so he was born into a comfortably off family.
- He went into the pawnbroking business in 1861 at the age of nineteen (possibly earlier) and by 1878 at the age of 36 he owned his first shop, freehold.
- He then worked his way up to becoming the owner of a thriving and profitable pawnbroking business, employing staff and at one time operating three shops in Hull city centre; in other words, he was driven to make his business successful.
- He was apparently regarded as a reputable businessman, being called upon to give character references for those applying for alehouse and pawnbroker's licences, and making several court appearances as a witness to and/or prosecutor in relation to thefts from his shops.
- By 1890 he was living in a large house in Coltman Street in west Hull, at that time a very respectable area.
- He retired at the early age of 56, after he sold his business to Owen and Robinson Ltd in 1898, this making him a very wealthy man.
- On retirement he moved to an even bigger house in Coltman Street, becoming part of a wealthy community of businessmen and "gentlemen".

- In his will, Collier himself was described as a "gentleman".
- On his death in 1913, he left an estate worth £4,297 17s 4d (£614,594.91), which included twelve smaller terraced houses which were tenanted, his own Coltman Street house, and many items of value such as gold and silver jewellery, paintings and antique furniture.

Some possible explanations for the unsolved mystery

In the light of Collier's apparent standing in both the business community and in his personal life (as described above), it is perhaps difficult to imagine that he would do something illegal or shady in his business, such as hiding pawn tickets up the chimney in his main shop in South Street; however, Collier's complete honesty cannot be established with any certainty, and nor can that of his various assistants over the years. Some possible explanations as to why these pawn tickets were hidden are outlined below; these are a product not only of the author's research but also of the many discussions about the mystery between the Carnegie volunteers including the author, and also of discussions between the author and various others. In addition, readers of this book might well come up with their own explanations, as the ones suggested below are by no means exhaustive. **If readers can suggest any other explanations, the author would be very interested to hear them, so please let her know via the Carnegie Heritage Centre (contact details on the back of this book).**

It is possible that Collier did not follow completely the stipulations of the 1872 Pawnbrokers Act (see above). Part of this act laid down the documentation and exact wording on it that pawnbrokers had to use in their business; it is known that at least in the span of years on the previously hidden tickets, Collier used the correct wording on the tickets (as described and pictured above), but it has already been pointed out that the 1898 prospectus for the sale of Collier's business and that of other pawnbrokers to Owen and Robinson Ltd stated that Collier had no proper book keeping system. The 1872 Act stated that there were penalties for not keeping proper records, so perhaps the transactions on the previously hidden pawn tickets had for whatever reason had gone unrecorded, hence them being hidden to avoid prosecution.

There is another possible explanation in connection with the 1898 sale of Collier's business to Owen and Robinson Ltd. The previously hidden pawn tickets are dated from 1887 to 1896, the latter being two years before this sale; it is possible that as early as 1896 Collier knew of Owen and Robinson Ltd's intentions to buy his business, as the sale would have involved time consuming negotiations, as well as valuations of Collier's South Street property, his stock and the profits he was making. Whilst preparing his paperwork and documentation for the sale, Collier could have hidden the pawn tickets up the chimney because they were not recorded properly; on the other hand, they might have been worth recording, as they would have added to the valuation of his profits. Having said that, at the time of the sale to Owen and Robinson Ltd Collier appears already to have been a wealthy man, so even the profit on the 6,871 previously hidden pawn tickets could have had little impact on the valuation of his business; in other words, Collier could easily afford to lose these profits.

Another possible explanation for the hidden pawn tickets which came up in several discussions was that that the items on the tickets were stolen goods. The 1872 Act made it an offence for a pawnbroker to offer loans on such goods, but it seems extremely unlikely that the many items recorded on the tickets were all stolen, particularly low value items such as handkerchiefs. By the same token, it would seem equally unlikely that Collier and/or his assistants took in all the items, either knowing or not knowing that they were stolen.

It could be that one of Collier's assistants hid the pawn tickets without his knowledge, because they had not recorded them properly; this could have been connected or unconnected to the sale of the business to Owen and Robinson Ltd. However, given the span of nine years on the tickets' dates, this can perhaps be considered unlikely (but not impossible) because of the possible turnover of employed staff in the business, meaning that more than one assistant was culpable. Equally unlikely is that an assistant hid the pawn tickets up the chimney because they had stolen the goods, as there are too many of them itemised on the tickets for this to be feasible. In a similar vein, if the items on the tickets were all unredeemed, Collier himself could have taken personal possession of them and sold them privately, without putting them through the books.

Finally, another possible explanation for the pawn tickets being hidden up the chimney is income tax evasion. In 1816 income tax was abandoned after strong public opposition, but in 1842 it was reintroduced by the then Prime Minister Sir Robert Peel. The tax was levied on those with an income of £150 (£21,450) a year, and the rate was 7d (£4.13) in the pound (£143) (UK Parliament, 2022a). As discussed above, in the 1898 prospectus for the sale of Collier's and other pawnbrokers' businesses to Owen and Robinson Ltd, Collier's annual profit and that of Hammond's business in Leeds were estimated together to be £750

(£107,250). For convenience, assuming that each of these two businesses made half of this annual profit i.e. £375 (£53,625), and equating profit with income, it appears that Collier would be liable for income tax, especially as he at one time had two other shops in Hull which would have boosted his profit. Although this calculation makes some assumptions, it is nevertheless a possible explanation as to why 6,871 pawn tickets were hidden up the chimney in Collier's South Street premises.

REFLECTIONS

The mystery remains unsolved as to why 6,871 pawn tickets, all around 130 years old and belonging to pawnbroker Robert Collier, were found hidden (apparently deliberately) as far up the chimney as possible in his premises at 13 South Street in the centre of Hull. Nevertheless, this remarkable discovery in mid-2020 by Steve Constable and his team of builders has proved to be an invaluable primary source of historical information, painting a unique and vivid picture of pawnbroking in Hull in the second half of the nineteenth century, as well as of the social and economic conditions at that time. The builders' discovery was the inspiration for this book, and the author hopes that in turn, the book will be enjoyed by those with an interest in the social and economic history of the period, in particular that of Hull and the life of its residents at that time.

APPENDIX: AN ANALYSIS OF THE INFORMATION ON THE 6,871 PAWN TICKETS THAT WERE HIDDEN UP THE CHIMNEY IN COLLIER'S SOUTH STREET PREMISES

As explained earlier in this book, a team of Carnegie Heritage Centre volunteers entered the information on the 6,871 previously hidden pawn tickets onto a spreadsheet, to allow the author to analyse this and feed her findings into the text of the book. This appendix looks at the detailed analysis of the information on the pawn tickets i.e. year of the transaction, the customer's surname, their address, the item(s) they pawned and the amount loaned to them by Collier on the item(s). There are several things to bear in mind when reading this analysis:

- The analysis is of the information on 6,871 pawn tickets dated from 1887 to 1896; as such it is a snapshot in time, and the findings of the analysis may not be representative of other periods of time, other pawnbrokers or other areas of the country.
- The Carnegie Heritage Centre volunteers who entered the information on the pawn tickets onto the spreadsheet were reading from 130 year

old handwritten originals, many of which were difficult to read, leaving the volunteers to make educated guesses as to what was written. In some cases even this was impossible, so the volunteers had to leave blanks on the spreadsheet. Here are two examples of such handwriting in photographs taken by Carnegie Heritage Centre volunteer Carol Broughton:

 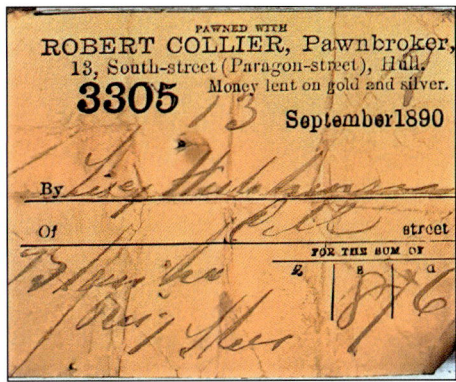

- To make the volunteers' task even more difficult, a few of the pawn tickets were damaged, so that some of the information on them was missing. In these cases the volunteers had to leave blanks on the spreadsheet. Here are two examples of damaged tickets, in a photograph taken by the author:

- The pawn tickets were very sooty when they were first found, having been hidden in the chimney stack above the coal fires at 13 South Street for around 130 years. Although the volunteers wiped off as much of the soot as possible, in some cases it had become ingrained, leading to some of the information on the tickets being unreadable; as with the damaged tickets, the volunteers had then to leave blanks on the spreadsheet. Here are two examples of tickets with ingrained soot on them, in a photograph taken by the author:

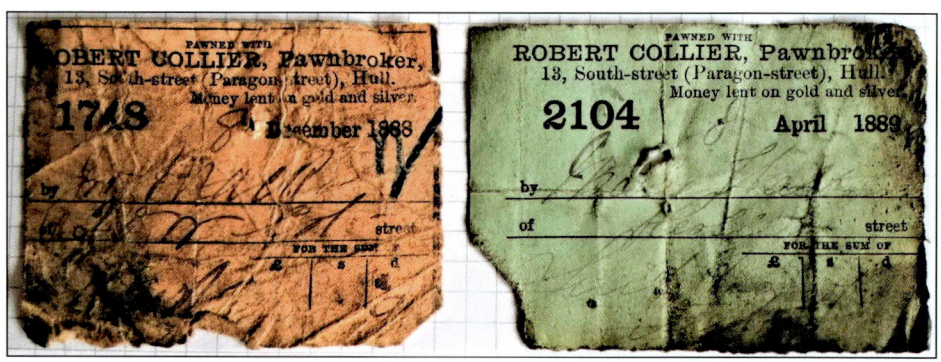

- A number of tickets did not have all the information on them, even though they were legible and/or undamaged; in these cases, the volunteers had to leave blanks on the spreadsheet.

These factors have led to a few inconsistencies in the figures quoted in the analysis below, but overall these do not detract greatly from the impact of the findings.

Analysis by year

As mentioned above, the pawn tickets dated from 1887 to 1896. The table below shows the distribution between these years.

YEAR	NO OF TICKETS	YEAR	NO OF TICKETS
1887	1	1893	489
1888	650	1894	53
1889	3,894	1895	5
1890	2,027	1896	119
1891	2	No Year	25
1892			

Approximately 96% (6,571 individual tickets) of the total number of tickets are from the years 1888, 1889 and 1890, with smaller peaks in 1893 and 1896.

Analysis by surname

Throughout this part of the analysis, it must be borne in mind that many of Collier's customers used his services more than once, so the surnames may be either the same person, or a different person or family. This is perhaps an indication that during the nine year range of dates on the pawn tickets, families were often either multi-generational and living in one house, and/or different branches of the same family living in their individual houses but near each other, especially in the overcrowded West End area of Hull adjacent to Collier's South Street shop (as described above).

The analysis by surname shows that there was a wide range of them amongst Collier's customers. Not unexpectedly, the most common ones on the pawn tickets were some of those still common today, for example Smith (134), Johnson (110) and Brown (97). The fourth most common surname on the pawn tickets was Wass (80), perhaps a more unusual name, but a good example of a repeat customer (in particular Ann Wass) or family. Other common surnames on the pawn tickets were Ward (75) and Robinson (59).

As mentioned above, there was an influx of workers into the cities during the second half of the nineteenth century. During this period many Irish people moved into Hull, and according to the pawn tickets there were quite a few people with Irish surnames using Collier's services. These included the Larking/Larkin (53, making this the seventh most common surname overall), the O'Briens/O'Brians (21), the Grogans (18), the Bolands (18), the Murphys (17) and the Conboys (15).

Analysis by address

The table overleaf shows the percentage of the total number of pawn tickets which had on them addresses in the areas indicated; these are the main areas which appeared on the pawn tickets, so are as such, they are not exhaustive.

In this table, the dominance of the West End in terms of where Collier's customers lived is plain to see. Also evident is the relatively small catchment area of Collier's South Street shop; the streets furthest away from the shop are Liverpool Street and Wassand Street, both off Hessle Road, which are approximately two miles away from South Street. There are a total of ten pawn tickets from these two streets, and it is interesting to speculate why these customers used Collier's South Street shop, when there were other pawn shops nearby, on Hessle Road itself. Despite using pawn shops being a way of life during the second half of the

AREA	STREETS	% OF TOTAL NO OF PAWN TICKETS
West End (described in detail earlier in this book, including a map of the West End)	West, South, Collier, Temperance, Moxon, Spencer, Spring, Mill, Garden, Middle, North, Chapel, Brook, Portland, Paragon, Chariot, Short and Canning Streets; Eastcheap	74% (of which 94% were West, South and Collier Streets)
Beverley Road and area	Beverley Road itself, Marlborough Terrace, Stepney Lane; Waterloo, Liddell, Norfolk, Francis and Derby Streets	2.19%
Hessle Road and area	Hessle Road itself; Glasgow, Liverpool, Wassand, William and Porter Streets	1.66%
Anlaby Road and area	Anlaby Road itself; Thornton, Bean, Campbell, English, Walker, Walton, Clarendon and Alexandra Streets	1.43%
Area east and north east of Carr Lane	Chariot, Medley, Waterworks, Edward, Story and Vincent Streets	0.65%
Osborne Street and area	Osborne Street itself, Great Passage Street and Waterhouse Lane	0.64%

nineteenth century (as discussed above), perhaps these customers felt a stigma pawning their possessions, so they went to a shop where their neighbours would be less likely to see them.

Analysis by item(s) pawned

The pawn tickets analysis shows that approximately 8,841 items were pawned; this is more than the total number of pawn tickets (6,871), because a proportion of the transactions were for multiple items on the same pawn ticket. When studying this part of the analysis, it must be borne in mind that some items may well have been repeatedly pawned, particularly by Collier's regular customers (see analysis by surname, above).

CATEGORIES	EXAMPLES OF ITEMS PAWNED	% OF TOTAL NO OF ITEMS PAWNED
Items of clothing	Trousers, coats, boots, vests, suits, shirts, jackets, gowns, aprons, shawls, drawers, skirts, nightgowns, cloaks, petticoats, stockings, dolmans (women's capes)	76%
Household items, excluding bedding (see below)	Flannels, tablecloths, cutlery, rugs, towels, cruet stands, toast racks, plates, biscuit box, kettle stand	10.3%
Jewellery	Rings (including 39 wedding, 31 keeper and 7 diamond), watches (including 55 silver and 21 gold), Alberts (pocket watches with chains, including 24 gold and 24 silver), brooches, earrings, gold chains, bracelets	7.5%
Bedding	Sheets, blankets, turnovers, counterpanes	3.6%

The top ten most pawned items have already been discussed above. The table on the previous page shows the percentage of the total number of items pawned in several broad categories, together with examples of items within those categories.

Items of clothing were by far the most common items pawned; as pointed out above, it may be that poorer people had relatively little to pawn except their clothes. However, the table also shows the wider range of items pawned. The jewellery category is particularly interesting, as it includes some expensive gold and silver items. It may be that these were pawned by people who were normally more comfortably off but had perhaps fallen on hard times; equally, some of these items may have been owned by poorer families and passed down from generation to generation.

Pawned items that do not fall into any of the above categories but were still pawned fairly regularly include handkerchiefs (190), hand hooks (26) and books (24). There were also 31 pawn tickets marked "stuff"; it can be speculated that the "stuff" included too many items to list on one small pawn ticket, or that the shop was busy at the time so "stuff" was used for expediency, or that the person behind the shop counter could not be bothered to write down multiple items!

It is also worth mentioning some of the more unusual items pawned: boas (4), concertinas (3), paper-hanging tools (2), guns (2), castors (2), a pencil case and a glazier's diamond.

Analysis by the amount loaned to the customer against the item(s)

In this part of the analysis, the point made above about the difficulty of reading the handwriting on 130 year old pawn tickets is especially pertinent, for example 8, 5 and 3 can look similar. It must also be borne in mind that some of the amounts loaned were for multiple items, and that approximately 671 pawn tickets had no amount on them.

The amounts loaned to Collier's customers ranged from 1d (59p) to £5 10s (£786.50). The table opposite shows the distribution of the amounts, as percentages of the total number of pawn tickets which have an amount on them (approximately 6,200).

The majority of the loans to Collier's customers were for amounts from 1s to 4s 11d (£7.15 to £35.09), the most common amount being 2s (£14.30), indicating that many of Collier's customers did not pawn items of any great value, and/or that they owned such items (as heirlooms, for example) but did not pawn them.

AMOUNT LOANED	% OF TOTAL NO OF PAWN TICKETS WHICH HAVE AN AMOUNT ON THEM
1d to 11d (0.59p to £6.49), most common amount 9d (£5.31)	3.2%
1s to 4s 11d (£7.15 to £35.09), most common amount 2s (£14.30)	62%
5s to 9s 11d (£35.75 to £70.84), most common amount 5s (£35.75)	19%
10s to 19s 11d (£71.50 to £142.34), most common amount 10s (£71.50)	6.4%
£1 to £5 10s (£143 to £785.50), most common amount £1 (£143)	1.3%

In terms of the wealth that Collier amassed during his lifetime (see above), the interest charged on all the items pawned in his three shops would have added up to a considerable amount. On top of that, there was the money Collier earned from selling unredeemed items, including the more valuable items he sold at auction or directly from his shops (as described above).

SOURCES USED

Aldridge, Carolyn. Images of 'Victorian' Hull: F.S. Smith's Drawings of the Old Town. Hull City Museums and Art Galleries and Hutton Press, 1989

Allison, K.J. (ed.). A History of the County of York East Riding: Volume 1, the City of Kingston-upon-Hull. https://www.british-history.ac.uk/vch/yorks/east/vol1 (originally published by Victoria County History, London, 1969)

Ancestry. https://www.ancestry.co.uk/ (used to access family records such as censuses and birth, marriage and death records)

Bowley, Arthur L. Wages in the United Kingdom in the Nineteenth Century: Notes for the Use of Students of Social and Economic Questions. Cambridge University Press, 1900. Wages in the United Kingdom in the nineteenth century (archive.org)

British Newspaper Archive. https://britishnewspaperarchive.co.uk (used primarily to access newspapers local to Hull)

Carnegie Heritage Centre: various resources, including street directories, books, maps and photographs

Facebook groups: Hull the Good Old Days, Hull Areas the Old Years, Hull and Yorkshire Memories, Hull Good Old Days, Hull Memories and Pictures, This is Old Hull, Hull Chat (all used primarily to find relevant photographs)

Find My Past. https://www.findmypast.co.uk/ (used to access family records such as censuses and birth, marriage and death records)

General Board of Health. Report on the Epidemic Cholera of 1848 & 1849. HMSO, 1850. 15-78-29A-22-1850-GBoH-MuckGarthsHull.pdf (msu.edu)

Gibson, Paul. Hull Then and Now 1. Carnegie Heritage Centre Action Team, 2008

Gibson, Paul. Hull Then and Now 4. Paul Gibson, 2013

Gillett, Edward and MacMahon, Kenneth A. A History of Hull. Hull University Press, 1980

Google Maps and Street View. https://www.maps.google.co.uk

Higgs, Michelle: Victorian Pawnbrokers. n.d. https://visitvictorianengland.com/2019/05/24/victorian-pawnbrokers/

Ketchell, Christopher. F.S. Smith's Drawings of Hull: Images of 'Victorian' Hull 2. Hull City Museums and Art Galleries and Hutton Press, 1990

Knowles, James (ed.) Life on a Guinea a Week. In *The Nineteenth Century: a Monthly Review* Issue 133 pp. 464 to 467. Kegan, Paul, Trench & Co, March 1888. The Cost of Living in 1888 (victorianweb.org)

LotSearch: Auction Search and Price Archive. n.d. www.lotsearch.net/artist/thomas-kirk/archive

Markham, John. Great Hull Stories. Fort Publishing, 2003

Markham, John. The Streets of Hull: a History of their Names. Highgate, 1987

Maxcroft Pawnbrokers. History of Pawnbroking. 2020. Pawnbrokers Through History | Immediate cash loans in London, Essex (maxcroft.co.uk)

McMahon, Craig M. The Regulation and Development of the British Moneylending and Pawnbroking Markets, 1870-2016: this dissertation is submitted for the degree of Doctor of Philosophy. University of Cambridge St. Edmund's College February 2018. cmcmahon cmm89 PhD Final (cam.ac.uk)

Muirhead, L. Russell, ed. The Blue Guides England. 5th edition. Benn, n.d. (map by Bartholomew and Son)

National Association of Pawnbrokers of the UK. n.d. https://www.thenpa.com

National Library of Scotland Maps. https://maps.nls.uk

National Probate Registry. https://www.gov.uk/search-will-probate

Pettingell, Frank N. Bird's Eye View of Hull, 1880. Search Results - Hull Museums Collections (hullcc.gov.uk)

Rosen, Dr Bruce. Victorian History: an Idiosyncratic Selection of Short Bits about Elements of Victorian History: Income vs Expenditure in Working Class Victorian England. n.d. Victorian History: Income vs Expenditure in Working-Class Victorian England (vichist.blogspot.com)

Smith, David Alexander. Forgotten Hull 3: a Selection of Photographs 1890s - 1930s. Kingston Press, 2012

UK Parliament. Income Tax Abolished and Reintroduced. UK Parliament, 2022a.

UK Parliament. The 1948 Public Health Act. UK Parliament, 2022b. The 1848 Public Health Act - UK Parliament

UK Parliament. The Public General Statutes Passed in the Thirty-Fifth and Thirty-Sixth Years of the Reign of Her Majesty Queen Victoria 1872: with a List of the Local and Private Acts, Tables Showing the Effect of the Year's Legislation, and a Copious Index. London: Queen's Printing Office, 1872. The_Public_General_Statutes_of_the_United_Kingdom_1872_(35_&_36_Victoria).pdf (wikimedia.org) [Note: the 1872 Pawnbrokers Act is Chapter 93 in this document, pp. 657-680]

Webster, Ian. United Kingdom Inflation Calculator, 25th August 2022. UK Inflation Calculator: GBP from 1751 to 2022 (in2013dollars.com)

Wikipedia Commons. https://commons.wikimedia.org/

Wikipedia. History of Pawnbroking, 2022. History of pawnbroking - Wikipedia [based on an article in the Encyclopaedia Britannica, 11th ed. 1910 to 1911]

Wilkinson, Graham. Forgotten Hull 2: a Selection of Photographs from the 1890s - 1930s. Kingston Press, 2000

Wilkinson, Graham and Watkins, Gareth. Forgotten Hull: a Selection of Photographs taken from the Hull Corporation Health Department Collection 1890s – 1930s. Kingston Press, 1999.

ACKNOWLEDGEMENTS

The author's thanks go to Steve Constable and his team of builders, who rather than destroy the pawn tickets they accidentally found hidden up the chimney in South Street, realised their historical significance and offered them to the Carnegie Heritage Centre. Without Steve and his team, this book would not have been written. Thanks are also due to one of Steve's team, Dean Paterson, who showed the author and a fellow Carnegie volunteer around the South Street premises in October 2020, pointing out the remaining original features of the building and where the pawn tickets had been found.

The Carnegie Heritage Centre volunteers who sorted out the 6,871 pawn tickets, cleaned them and entered the information on them onto a spreadsheet deserve the author's grateful thanks for the hours of work they put in on this dirty, difficult and time consuming task. It must also be said that the volunteers found the tickets so fascinating that much productive discussion was engendered about them, not only adding value to the author's research, but also making the sorting and entering process even longer, but in a good way! Thanks also to volunteer Keith Mawer at the Carnegie Heritage Centre for reading the draft of this book and putting me right where necessary, to volunteer Carol Broughton for photographs of the pawn tickets, and to Liz Shepherd for her encouragement during the writing of this book. Thanks too to Bill and Jeanne Longbone of the Friends of Hull General Cemetery, who identified the graves of Robert Collier and Elizabeth Dunlin and the monumental inscriptions on the long gone headstones. Last but by no means least, the author's thanks go to Paul Gibson for allowing the use of his photographs in this book.

THE AUTHOR

Christine Pinder was born in Hull and has spent her whole life in the city, apart from four years away at university. Her career was in librarianship and study skills teaching, both in higher education. Christine retired in 2012 and has since developed a keen interest in local and family history, largely due to her volunteering activities at the Carnegie Heritage Centre in Hull, where she has catalogued the books and maps collections. Christine now undertakes local history research not only for the Carnegie Heritage Centre and its customers, but also for other voluntary organisations such as the Hull and Barnsley Railway Stock Fund and the Old Kingstonians' Association, both based largely in Hull. Her research has been published in the newsletters of these organisations.

Christine wrote this book as a volunteer at the Carnegie Heritage Centre in Hull. The Centre has extensive resources for local, family and military historians. Although based in Hull, the volunteers undertake research for people all over the world. The Centre is based in a Grade 2 listed building built in 1905 in an Arts and Crafts style, and situated at the gates of West Park on Anlaby Road in Hull. It is managed and run entirely by volunteers with the support of Hull City Council, who let the building to the group at a peppercorn rent. All other costs are covered by the organisation through sales of books such as this.